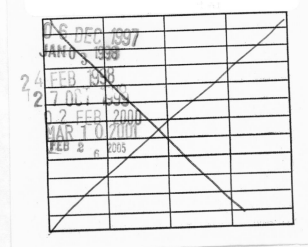

THE IMPORTANCE OF

Tecumseh

These and other titles are included in The Importance
Of biography series:

Alexander the Great	Harry Houdini
Muhammad Ali	Thomas Jefferson
Louis Armstrong	Mother Jones
James Baldwin	Chief Joseph
Clara Barton	Joe Louis
Napoleon Bonaparte	Malcolm X
Julius Caesar	Thurgood Marshall
Rachel Carson	Margaret Mead
Charlie Chaplin	Michelangelo
Charlemagne	Wolfgang Amadeus Mozart
Cesar Chavez	John Muir
Winston Churchill	Sir Isaac Newton
Cleopatra	Richard M. Nixon
Christopher Columbus	Georgia O'Keeffe
Hernando Cortes	Louis Pasteur
Marie Curie	Pablo Picasso
Amelia Earhart	Elvis Presley
Thomas Edison	Jackie Robinson
Albert Einstein	Norman Rockwell
Duke Ellington	Anwar Sadat
Dian Fossey	Margaret Sanger
Benjamin Franklin	Oskar Schindler
Galileo Galilei	John Steinbeck
Emma Goldman	Tecumseh
Jane Goodall	Jim Thorpe
Martha Graham	Mark Twain
Stephen Hawking	Queen Victoria
Jim Henson	Pancho Villa
Adolf Hitler	H. G. Wells

THE IMPORTANCE OF

Tecumseh

by
Myra H. and William H. Immell

Lucent Books, P.O. Box 289011, San Diego, CA 92198-9011

Library of Congress Cataloging-in-Publication Data

Immell, Myra.
    The importance of Tecumseh / by Myra H. and William
H. Immell.
        p.   cm. — (The importance of)
    Includes bibliographical references and index.
    Summary: Presents the life of the Shawnee chief, states-
man, orator, warrior, and diplomat who attempted to unite
the different Native American groups into one Indian
nation.
    ISBN 1-56006-087-5 (alk. paper)
    1. Tecumseh, Shawnee Chief, 1768–1813—Juvenile litera-
ture. 2. Shawnee Indians—Kings and rulers—Biography—
Juvenile literature.   3. Shawnee Indians—History. 4. Shawnee
Indians—Government relations. [1. Tecumseh, Shawnee
Chief, 1768–1813. 2. Shawnee Indians—Biography. 3. Indians
of North America—Biography.]   I. Immell, William H.,
1940–   . II. Series.
E99.S35.T155   1997
973'.04973'0092—dc21
    [B]   96–51518
                                                           CIP
                                                            AC

Copyright 1997 by Lucent Books, Inc., P.O. Box 289011,
San Diego, California 92198-9011

Printed in the U.S.A.

Contents

Foreword

THE IMPORTANCE OF biography series deals with individuals who have made a unique contribution to history. The editors of the series have deliberately chosen to cast a wide net and include people from all fields of endeavor. Individuals from politics, music, art, literature, philosophy, science, sports, and religion are all represented. In addition, the editors did not restrict the series to individuals whose accomplishments have helped change the course of history. Of necessity, this criterion would have eliminated many whose contribution was great, though limited. Charles Darwin, for example, was responsible for radically altering the scientific view of the natural history of the world. His achievements continue to impact the study of science today. Others, such as Chief Joseph of the Nez Percé, played a pivotal role in the history of their own people. While Joseph's influence does not extend much beyond the Nez Percé, his nonviolent resistance to white expansion and his continuing role in protecting his tribe and his homeland remain an inspiration to all.

These biographies are more than factual chronicles. Each volume attempts to emphasize an individual's contributions both in his or her own time and for posterity. For example, the voyages of Christopher Columbus opened the way to European colonization of the New World. Unquestionably, his encounter with the New World brought monumental changes to both Europe and the Americas in his day. Today, however, the broader impact of Columbus's voyages is being critically scrutinized. *Christopher Columbus,* as well as every biography in The Importance Of series, includes and evaluates the most recent scholarship available on each subject.

Each author includes a wide variety of primary and secondary source quotations to document and substantiate his or her work. All quotes are footnoted to show readers exactly how and where biographers derive their information, as well as provide stepping stones to further research. These quotations enliven the text by giving readers eyewitness views of the life and times of each individual covered in The Importance Of series.

Finally, each volume is enhanced by photographs, bibliographies, chronologies, and comprehensive indexes. For both the casual reader and the student engaged in research, The Importance Of biographies will be a fascinating adventure into the lives of people who have helped shape humanity's past and present, and who will continue to shape its future.

IMPORTANT DATES IN THE LIFE OF TECUMSEH

1763
The British forbid white settlement west of the Appalachians; Ottawa chief Pontiac leads Indian uprising against the British

1768
Tecumseh is born March 9 in village of Piqua on Mad River

1774
Tecumseh's father, Pucksinwah, is killed by whites in the Battle of Point Pleasant; Shawnee chief Cornstalk signs treaty recognizing Ohio River as southern boundary of Shawnee territory

1775–1783
British and Americans fight War of Independence (American Revolution)

1783
British and Americans sign Treaty of Paris

1789
Tecumseh travels among Missouri and Illinois Shawnee, Miami, Kickapoo, Creek, and Cherokee; Chiksika is killed by whites on Tennessee frontier

1794
Tecumseh and Miami chief Little Turtle attack Fort Recovery; Americans led by General Anthony Wayne defeat Indians at Battle of Fallen Timbers on Maumee River

1795
Chiefs representing twelve tribes sign Greenville treaty, giving Americans much Indian land

1796
Tecumseh marries Mohnetohse and their son Mahyawwekawpawe is born; Tecumseh marries Mamate

1797
Mamate gives birth to Tecumseh's son Naythawaynah

1805
Tecumseh's younger brother Low-

awluwaysica becomes Tenskwatawa, the Prophet, a powerful religious leader

1807
Tecumseh speaks at council in Chillicothe and meets with Ohio governor and other U.S. officials

1808
Tecumseh and Tenskwatawa establish Prophetstown; Tecumseh begins four years of travels among tribes from Missouri down to Florida

1809
Chiefs of the Miami, Delaware, Potawatomi, and other Indian nations sign Treaty of Fort Wayne, giving millions of acres of Indian land to the United States

1810
Tecumseh and the Prophet meet with Governor Harrison at Vincennes

1811
Tecumseh visits western Michigan, then eastern and southeastern Indian nations, to urge them to join his confederacy; New Madrid earthquake occurs, in accordance with a recent prediction by Tecumseh; Harrison defeats Prophet's followers at Battle of Tippecanoe and destroys Prophetstown; Tecumseh exiles Prophet

1812
Tecumseh and followers side with Great Britain against United States as the War of 1812 begins; troops led by Tecumseh and British general Isaac Brock capture Detroit; General Brock is succeeded by Henry Proctor

1813
Braves massacre Kentuckians at River Raisin; troops led by Tecumseh and General Proctor besiege Fort Meigs; Proctor retreats from Americans after Battle of Lake Erie; Tecumseh is killed in Canada at Battle of the Thames

"I Shall Stamp on the Ground with My Foot"

At 2 A.M. on December 16, 1811, in New Madrid, Missouri—a village on the Mississippi River about sixty miles below the mouth of the Ohio River—an earthquake struck. It was an earthquake unlike any other:

> They heard rumbling sounds, like distant thunder fast approaching, soon followed by deafening explosions sounding like large cannon. Mixed with the rumblings and sharp explosions was an earsplitting roar, accompanied by a loud hissing and a shrill whistling sound, all emanating [coming] from the ground. . . .
>
> Flashes of bright light suddenly burst from the earth, which shook violently. . . . In places, it rolled and undulated [rose and fell] in waves. As the waves peaked, the earth burst open and spewed forth water, sand, rock, and coal, often as high as the treetops. . . . Everywhere, the ground shook furiously from side to side. . . .
>
> The ground throughout the town began to sink, and a black liquid oozed from the earth, rising eventually to a depth of three feet. Large fissures [cracks] opened, splitting the ground into hundreds of deep chasms, some of them seven feet wide and of untold depth. . . .
>
> The trees in the nearby forests waved frantically. Many were split up the middle as fissures opened beneath them. Oak trees, sometimes split to a height of forty feet, perched precariously [unsecurely], one half on one side of a fissure, the other on the other side. . . . Thousands of trees, whole forests, fell in unison. . . .
>
> In the town itself, most of the houses had been thrown down in piles of rubble by the time the Mississippi River overflowed its banks and began to flood the town. The town's cemetery and its dead were exposed and carried away by torrents of water. . . . Each succeeding shake knocked down everything and everyone that was standing.[1]

By 7 o'clock that morning, there had been at least twenty-seven shocks, and New Madrid was no longer. By the time the worst was over, the earthquake had been felt in at least twenty-seven states, from Alabama to Ohio to Connecticut to Vermont.

The shocks came and went, off and on, for two days. The next month, just when people were getting over the first shock, two more hit. And on February 13,

As Tecumseh had predicted, a devastating earthquake struck New Madrid, Missouri, on December 16, 1811. The powerful quake caused the Mississippi River to flood the small village and sent shock waves into at least twenty-seven other states.

1812, there was another one, which lasted an hour—a shock so bad that it did as much damage as all the ones before.

The earthquake had taken most people by surprise—but not quite everyone. Some North American Indians knew an earthquake would come. Nine years before, a Shawnee named Tecumseh had predicted it. Working to unite his people, he had said that a sign would come from the heavens as proof that the supreme god Moneto wanted them to unite. When Moneto was ready, he told them, the earth would tremble and shake so hard that great forests would fall, streams would run uphill, and rivers would escape their chan-

nels. The sign would be so violent that people could not help but feel it, and they never would be able to forget it.

More recently—in October 1811—just two months before the huge earthquake actually hit, Tecumseh was in Tuckhabatchee, a Creek village in Alabama on the west bank of the Tallapoosa River. There, some five hundred Indians had gathered in council to listen to him talk to the Upper Creek chief Menawa—"Big Warrior." Tecumseh wanted Menawa to join with him in a confederation of all North American Indians. Such a confederation, proclaimed the Shawnee, could stand up to the whites who were taking over Indian lands. Menawa had a lot of influence, so it was important to have his support.

At first, Menawa pretended to approve. Pleased, Tecumseh gave him special gifts to symbolize his allegiance to the confederation—a bundle of red sticks, a tomahawk, and a form of currency known as wampum. After he had accepted the gifts, however, Menawa stopped pretending. He would not, he told Tecumseh, give his seal of approval to the confederation. Tecumseh was furious. Looking Menawa right in the eye, Tecumseh insulted and threatened him:

> "Your blood is white," the Shawnee said defiantly. "You have taken my talk, and the sticks, and the wampum, and the hatchet, but you do not mean to fight. I know the reason. You do not believe the Great Spirit has sent me. You shall know. I leave Tuckhabatchee directly—and shall go straight to Detroit. When I arrive there, I shall stamp on the ground with my foot, and shake down every house in Tuckhabatchee."[2]

Having spoken these words, Tecumseh turned and left.

Once Tecumseh had gone, Menawa and his braves began to worry. They figured out just how many days it would take Tecumseh to get to Detroit. The closer it got to that day, the more nervous they became. Finally, the day they were waiting for arrived. And with it came a mighty rumbling. It was the day of the great New Madrid earthquake. With the earth shaking beneath them, they ran out of their homes, which, just as Tecumseh had warned, were falling down one after another. Also as Tecumseh had predicted,

before it was over not one was left standing. Tecumseh had stamped his foot, and the sign that the great Shawnee leader had predicted would unite all North American Indians had come on the exact day he said it would. Convinced of Tecumseh's power and the wisdom of his

Tecumseh, the great Shawnee leader, warrior, and orator, dedicated his life to uniting the North American Indians against the encroachment of whites.

confederacy, warriors picked up their weapons and headed out to join him in his fight.

Tecumseh devoted his life to trying to make sure his people's rights and freedoms were respected and the North American Indian way of life would be preserved. Wise beyond his years, he was a statesman, an orator, a warrior, and a diplomat. He dedicated his all to bringing together the many different Native American groups, attempting to unite them in one Indian nation strong enough to protect and preserve what was rightfully theirs. A fearless and determined leader, Tecumseh worked to instill in his people a strong sense of integrity, humanity, justice, and a will to fight against outrageous odds. Many people today believe he was the greatest of all the remarkable chiefs to have emerged during the long struggle of the Indian Wars.

1 Night of the Panther Passing Over

At exactly the moment Tecumseh was born, on the night of March 9, 1768, the fiery trail of a great meteor streaked across the sky. To some, this was a sign that the baby was meant for greatness.

The Shawnee

Tecumseh was born a Shawnee, part of the Algonquin family of Native Americans known as "southerners." They were a proud, fierce people, the "most competent woodsmen, greatest hunters, fiercest warriors, and among the most intelligent Indians on the American continent."[3] For some, they were "the most warlike, persistent, and consistently hostile of the nations. The mention of the name Shawnee suggests aggression, restlessness, and fearlessness."[4]

The Shawnee themselves thought that they were better than any other Indians in character and in origin. As one Shawnee chief explained:

The Master of Life was himself an Indian. He made the Shawanoes before any other Indian race. They sprang from his brain. He gave them all the knowledge he possessed and placed them upon the great island, and all the other red people descended from the Shawanoes. After these he made the French and the English out of his breast, the Dutch out of his feet and the Long Knives [the Americans] out of his hands. All of these inferior races of men he made white and placed them beyond the stinking lake [Atlantic Ocean].[5]

The Way of Life

The Shawnee were hunters and gatherers who lived off the riches of the land. They also raised crops and, by the time Tecumseh was born, had begun to trade with the whites. They built their villages and towns around a large log council house that they usually used for ceremonies.

Each Shawnee village was home to about three hundred people, and all were much the same. Men hunted and tracked. The buffalo was a favorite prey because it had so many uses. Its meat could be eaten fresh, or dried and mixed with fat and berries and stored for the winter months. Its skin could be tanned and used for bedding and for the walls of the tepees the Shawnee lived in when they traveled.

A Unique Shawnee Tradition

Each Indian nation has its own story and beliefs about its origins. In the 1800s, in their History of the Indian Tribes of North America, *James Hall and J. L. McKenney quoted Benjamin Drake's explanation of what the Shawnee believed about their origin.*

"There is a tradition among the Shawanoes, in regard to their origin, which is said to be peculiar to their tribe. While most of the aborigines [natives] of this country believe that their respective races came out of holes in the earth at different places in this continent, the Shawanoes alone claim that their ancestors once inhabited a foreign land; but having determined to leave it, they assembled their people and marched to the sea shore. Here, under the guidance of a leader of the Turtle tribe, one of their twelve original subdivisions, they walked into the sea, the waters of which immediately parted, and they passed in safety along the bottom of the ocean, until they reached this island."

While the men looked for game, Shawnee women farmed and cooked, growing and preparing in different ways such crops as beans, squash, pumpkin, and corn. Children were well loved—and well disciplined. They were not allowed to run wild, whine, or make needless noise. They were taught to respect their elders and were reminded often that good conduct would earn a reward and evil conduct would bring sorrow. Spreading gossip about another person, they were told, was a crime. And, above all, as Shawnee, the only thing they owed people of other races was to return in kind the treatment they received. There were no schools. Children learned by doing. Boys were told or shown what to do by the men of the village, while girls received their instructions from female tribal members. Even though both boys and girls were treated kindly and with care, most Shawnee parents wanted to have more sons than daughters. Firstborn sons received a lot of special attention.

Shawnee lives were tied to the land, so day-to-day life was tied to the seasons. Thus there were summer towns, in which the Shawnee lived from March through August, and winter towns, in which they lived from late August or September until March.

South of the summer town, the men cleared the land. They burnt down the trees and used the ashes for fertilizer. In April the women tilled the soil and planted corn, squash, pumpkins, and beans. Later in the season, they harvested these crops. The last harvest was in August. Right afterward, everyone except those who were very sick or very old moved on to the winter town, or camp—a more protected place, a sheltered valley perhaps, where the men could begin their winter hunt. Sometimes the people of a really large village split up into bands. Each band went off on its own to find a place to make camp. Once a band had made camp, there the people stayed until it was time to move back to the summer town. From the time the camp was made until December, the men hunted game—deer, buffalo, bear, wild turkey. Then, from December to February, they trapped small animals such as raccoons.

For many years, the Shawnee dressed plainly. They used feathers, porcupine quills, and bits and pieces of shell to decorate their clothes and their deerskin moccasins. Owl, hawk, and eagle feathers rose from their headbands. Later, after they began trading with whites, they wore blankets, calico shirts, silver brooches, and brightly colored strands of ribbons. Sometimes, after Shawnee braves had won a battle, they wore the uniforms of the white army officers they had killed or taken prisoner, using the buttons and rings as jewelry.

On the Move

Many Algonquin peoples stayed in one area. But not the Shawnee. Over time they fanned out across the eastern half of the United States, spreading out across fifteen states. In the 1740s, about twenty years before Tecumseh was born, other Indian nations drove the Shawnee from their settlements in Georgia and the Carolinas. In the period that followed, the Shawnee wandered through the gap of the Cumberland Mountains of Tennessee, then on to the Susquehanna Mountains of Pennsylvania, over the hunting grounds of Kentucky.

In 1763 the British declared a boundary that for the most part ran north and south, following the crest of the Appalachian Mountains. They told the Indians to stay west of the imaginary line and warned whites not to settle or take up land in the region assigned to the Indians. Five years later—the year Tecumseh was born—the British persuaded Iroquois and

The Shawnee Indians, like their Algonquin relatives, lived in wigwams consisting of a dome-shaped framework of poles covered with tree bark, rush mats, or animal hides.

Cherokee chiefs to sign a treaty agreeing that whites could have lands west of the 1763 boundary. Neither the Cherokee nor the Iroquois lived on the land their chiefs signed away. It was the home of the Delaware and the Shawnee. Forced to move off the land and beyond the Ohio River, the Shawnee migrated toward the Scioto River in Ohio and formed a settlement at the Mad River, where fish and game were plentiful. Here the Shawnee prospered and grew. They became the largest Indian nation in Ohio.

A Meteor Lights the Sky

Here on the Mad River, not many miles southwest of present-day Springfield, Ohio, Tecumseh was born in the village of Piqua—"village that rises from its ashes." His father was a Shawnee warrior from Florida named Pucksinwah—"One Who Drops Down." His mother was Pucksinwah's second wife, a Cherokee from Alabama named Methotasa—"A Turtle Laying Her Eggs in the Sand." Three years later, Methotasa had triplets. One of them grew up to become both Tecumseh's strongest ally and his worst enemy—the Prophet.

Tecumseh was born into the warrior clan of the Shawnee—the Kispokotha. It was one of five major Shawnee divisions, or clans, each with its own peace chief and war chief. The chiefs of each of the clans owed allegiance to the head chief of all the Shawnee. They made decisions that affected all Shawnee in a council led by the head chief and advised by elders.

According to Shawnee custom relating to boy babies, Tecumseh—"Panther Passing Across"—was not named until he was ten days old. His name reflected the passing of the meteor and showed that he belonged to the Great Lynx clan of the Shawnee. His identity, like that of all Shawnee, was tied to a trait or characteris-

While living in the winter camp, Shawnee men hunted buffalo and other game. When the Shawnee were driven from their homelands, they migrated to new hunting grounds and eventually settled in Ohio.

tic of one of twelve different groups of animals that included the raccoon, the panther, the deer, the rabbit, and the wolf.

The Whites, the Land, and Revenge

By the time Tecumseh was a few years old, white settlers were pouring into Shawnee land south of the Ohio River. Since 1763, no matter what the whites had done, the Shawnee had kept the peace and stayed at home on the land the British had said was theirs. But their patience came to an end in 1774, when Virginians began to cross the Ohio and invade Shawnee land.

On October 10 of that year the mighty Shawnee chieftain Hokolesqua—"Cornstalk"—tried to defend the Scioto Valley. He launched a surprise attack against the British at Point Pleasant, where the Kanawha River empties into the Ohio River. Among the thousand or so warriors who rode with him were Tecumseh's father, Pucksinwah, and Tecumseh's older brother Chiksika. Cornstalk and his warriors fought a hard and bloody battle, but they did not win. As a result, Cornstalk signed a peace treaty that made the Ohio River a boundary between the Shawnee and the whites. The whites got all the Shawnee land south of the Ohio River, which meant that whites could now settle in Kentucky. But, said the treaty, no whites would try to settle on Shawnee land to the north of the river. Cornstalk kept his end of the bargain. The whites did not. They kept coming, invading more and more Shawnee territory in Ohio, pushing the Shawnee off their own land.

Pucksinwah did not survive the Battle of Point Pleasant. He was killed by a rifle

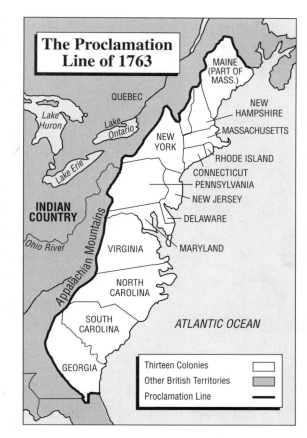

ball in the chest during the battle. Chiksika saw him fall and tried to plug up the wound. But it was too late. Before Pucksinwah died, he made Chiksika promise to take care of Tecumseh, teach him to be a good warrior and man, and guide him in the right way. He also begged Chiksika to provide for the family and never to make peace with the *Shamanese*—the Long Knives, as the Shawnee called Americans. Weeping, Chiksika gave his word.

A few months after Pucksinwah was killed, Chiksika brought his mother, his sister Tecumapese, Tecumseh, the triplets, and their adopted brother Blue Jacket to the household of his father's friend Chiungalla—"Black Fish." Chiungalla was a

A Shooting Star

A spectacular event took place on the night Tecumseh was born. With these words, Pulitzer Prize–winning writer-historian Allan Eckert tells in his work The Frontiersmen *what Tecumseh's father saw that night and what it meant to Tecumseh's parents.*

"He raised his eyes skyward but the prayer died aborning as a huge meteor suddenly plunged into the atmosphere and burst into brilliant greenish-white flame. It streaked across the heavens from the north in an awe-inspiring spectacle which lasted fully twenty seconds.

Pucksinwah had heard of such occurrences, but not before had he seen anything so breathtaking as this and the tales of the old people came back to him now: this shooting star was The Panther, a great spirit passing over to the south where it seeks a hole for sleep. Every night it passes somewhere on the earth to go to that home in the south. It was a good sign indeed and Pucksinwah arose and stepped briskly to the fire where the women were clustered, chattering excitedly, for they too had seen it.

From within the temporary shelter came the sharp wail of a baby. Pucksinwah waited quietly, the murmur of voices from inside almost lost in the gurgle of water from the great bubbling spring beside the shelter. Soon the infant's crying faded away and a quarter hour later one of the women came out, beckoned the chief and happily told him he had a son. . . .

Methotasa smiled up at Pucksinwah as he knelt to look at the baby. She told him that the other women had seen a great star, The Panther, passing across and searching for its home in the south. Pucksinwah nodded gravely and told her it was the boy child's *unsoma.*

Shawnee custom declares that a boy baby is not named for ten days after his birth, nor a girl for twelve, during which time an *unsoma*—notable event—would occur which should indicate what [the god] Moneto wished the child to be called. But this time the sign had been given at the very moment of birth and this was of great importance. Both Pucksinwah and Methotasa knew there could be no other name for this boy than The-Panther-Passing-Across."

chief in the main Shawnee village of Cha-lahgawtha, Old Chillicothe, which sat on the Mad River just south of Piqua. It was Shawnee custom that when a father was killed in battle, everyone helped the widow raise her children and another older man became their foster father.

Methotasa never got over the loss of her husband. According to legend, she swore revenge for Pucksinwah's death and told Tecumseh that he must become a warrior like his father—"a fire spreading over the hill and valley, consuming the race of dark souls."[6] Each year on the an-niversary of the day of Pucksinwah's mur-der, she took Tecumseh to visit his father's grave. She sang songs of revenge, made predictions, and filled her young son with a bitter hatred of whites.

Soon Methotasa was leaving the care of her younger children in the hands of her oldest daughter, Tecumapese. Two years younger than Chiksika and ten years older than Tecumseh, Tecumapese was like a mother to Tecumseh. She taught him that expressing emotions openly was a sign of weakness, that it was wrong to lie

or cheat, and that it was important to have compassion for the weak and the helpless. Tecumapese made her little brother un-derstand that nothing was more important than honor to a Shawnee brave.

Chiksika, meanwhile, kept the prom-ises he had made to his dying father. He educated his younger brother in the ways of their people and taught him how to be a Shawnee warrior. Since the Shawnee had no written language, they preserved their history by passing it from one generation to another by word of mouth. Chiksika told Tecumseh the tales of Shawnee history, making him repeat them over and over again until he knew them by heart. Many a night was spent by the campfire learning the deeds of ancestors and how the whites had wronged the Indian nations:

> It was we [went one story] who so kindly received the white men on their first arrival in this country. We took them by the hand and bid them wel-come to set down by our side and live with us as brothers. But how did they requite [repay] our kindness? They at

Although the Proclamation Line of 1763 gave the Indians the land west of the Appalachian Mountains, white settlers from Virginia and other colonies continued to pour into Shawnee land, establishing frontier communities.

During the Revolutionary War, the British recruited Native Americans in their fight against the colonists. Here, bow-and-arrow-carrying Indians encounter the Long Knives.

first asked for only a little land on which to raise bread for their families and pasture for their cattle. This we freely gave them. They saw the game in our woods, which the Great Spirit had given us for our subsistence and they wanted it, too. They penetrated into the woods in quest of game and discovered spots of land which they also wanted, and because we were loth [unwilling] to part with it, they took it from us by force and drove us a great distance from our homes.[7]

Drumbeats of War

By 1775 it was no longer just *Shamanese* against the Indian. Whites were fighting whites. Americans wanted freedom from British rule and were willing to make war to get it. The Shawnee and the other Indian nations could not escape the fighting. The drumbeat of the war echoed in the forests and across the prairies. The British, eager to have the Native Americans on their side, promised that if they won the war they would not take Indian land as the colonists had done.

Years before, Cornstalk had given his word that the Shawnee would not fight the Americans. But, as the atmosphere grew more warlike and tense, he could not control all of his people. In 1777, as a matter of honor, Cornstalk rode to warn the Long Knives of a Shawnee attack on some white settlements, an attack he had been unable to stop. His son and another Shawnee, Red Hawk, went with him. Cornstalk explained to the captain at the fort why they were there. They had barely finished speaking when they were taken hostage and locked in a small cabin. Before long they heard loud voices outside and saw a mob ready to attack the cabin. Cornstalk and his son stood their ground, but Red Hawk climbed up into the chimney. Even after the soldiers and frontiersmen had killed the two Shawnee, they kept on shooting bullets into them. Then they went after Red Hawk. They pulled him kicking and

Words of Warning

In his biography of Tecumseh, A Sorrow in Our Heart: The Life of Tecumseh, *historian Allan W. Eckert quotes Tecumseh's older brother Chiksika, who explained in 1779 how he felt about the Long Knives and how justice was different for them and for the Indian.*

"When a white man kills an Indian in a fair fight it is called honorable, but when an Indian kills a white man in a fair fight it is called murder. When a white army battles Indians and wins it is called a great victory, but if they lose it is called a massacre and bigger armies are raised. If the Indian flees before the advance of such armies, when he tries to return he finds that white men are living where he lived. If he tries to fight off such armies, he is killed and the land is taken anyway. When an Indian is killed it is a great loss which leaves a gap in our people and a sorrow in our heart; when a white is killed, three or four others step up to take his place and there is no end to it. The white man seeks to conquer nature, to bend it to his will and to use it wastefully until it is all gone and then he simply moves on, leaving the waste behind him and looking for new places to take. The whole white race is a monster who is always hungry and what he eats is land."

Indians flee as armies of white men approach. Although they would lose their land by leaving the village, the Indians would surely be killed if they stayed.

fighting out of his hiding place, shot him, tomahawked him, and with clubs and rifle butts beat him to a pulp.

There was no way for Indians to stay neutral, even if they wanted to. And most did not want to. The Shawnee wanted revenge for the murders of Cornstalk, his son, and Red Hawk. When, in 1778, the Americans destroyed Shawnee villages as far north as the Sandusky River, the anger of the Shawnee grew even greater. They knew that it was only a matter of time until the war came to Tecumseh's villages of Piqua and Chillicothe.

Chapter

2 From Boyhood to Manhood

In 1780 the Americans brought the war to Piqua and to Chillicothe. Determined not to let the Long Knives take their main village, the Shawnee burned Chillicothe to the ground. Finding this settlement in ashes, the Americans moved on to Piqua. But once again the Shawnee had outsmarted them. Piqua was deserted. The angry and tired Kentuckians and Virginians, led by Major General Roger Clark, torched the empty village.

War Games and Friendship

Tecumseh was now twelve years old. A quick and eager learner, he had mastered many of the skills taught to him by his brother Chiksika and his foster father Black Fish. He especially enjoyed war games. He knew that war was a serious matter and that even though the Shawnee were great fighters, they did not go to war lightly. He had

An Indian woman and her children abandon their home while the Long Knives set fire to their village.

Always the Leader

Stephen Ruddell, who grew up with Tecumseh, wrote a book about him. It is quoted in The Heroes of Defeat *by William Jackson Armstrong. In this excerpt, Ruddell portrays the young Tecumseh.*

"From his earliest boyhood he seemed to have a passion for war; his pastimes, like those of Napoleon, were generally in the sham battlefield; he was the leader of his companions in all their sports and was accustomed to divide them into parties, one of which he always headed for the purpose of fighting mimic battles in which he usually distinguished himself by his dexterity, strength, and skill; his dexterity in the use of the bow exceeded that of all other Indian boys of his tribe, by whom he was loved and respected and over whom he exercised an unbounded influence."

been taught that revenge and fishing, hunting, and farming rights were the main reasons to put on the red paint of war. But a Shawnee boy had to find some way to test his courage. What better way than fighting and war games? In the games the enemy was always the same—the *Shamanese*—and Tecumseh always wanted to be the leader. He knew that his fate was to become an even greater leader and warrior than his father or his older brother.

Tecumseh could hardly believe it when Chiksika told him that they both were going with the British to attack the Kentucky settlements. Their first target was Ruddell's Station on the Licking River. There, Chiksika and Tecumseh caught a young white boy, Stephen Ruddell, trying to escape. They took him with them on the rest of the campaign and then brought him home with them to the new village of Chillicothe that the Shawnee built to replace the one they had burned down. Chiksika was so impressed by the boy that he adopted him. Because the boy had been as slippery as a fish when they first tried to catch him, they gave him the Shawnee name Sinnantha— "Big Fish."

Sinnantha and Tecumseh became close friends. Tecumseh taught the white boy Shawnee ways and the Shawnee language. In return, Sinnantha taught Tecumseh English and helped him understand whites better. Tecumseh still did not like or approve of whites, but at least he knew a little more about them and why they acted the way they did. Sinnantha stayed with the group for fifteen years and married a Shawnee. In 1822, when he had resumed using the name Stephen Ruddell, he recalled in a letter:

I became acquainted with Tecumseh at the age of 12 years, and, being the same age as myself, we became inseparable companions. Tecumseh was always remarkable from his boyhood on for his dignity and behavior. There was something in his countenance [face] and manner that commanded respect and at the same time made those around him fond of him. During his boyhood, he used to place himself at the head of the youngsters and divide them and direct them in sham [make-believe] battles in which he would distinguish himself by his strength and skill.[8]

Treaties and Betrayals

In 1782 the British and the Americans signed a treaty making the Mississippi River the western boundary of the new United States. The British gave to their former colonies the lands claimed by Britain south of the Great Lakes and west of the Appalachian Mountains. This was a big blow to the Indian nations in the Northwest Territory—Ohio, Indiana, Illinois, Michigan, and Wisconsin. The land they were living on now belonged to the United States of America, and many Americans did not like them and would long remember that they had fought on the British side during the war.

The Indians felt angry and betrayed. They had helped the British when the British asked for assistance against the rebellious colonies. True, the British had lost the war. But they still had soldiers on U.S. land, at Detroit, Niagara, Oswego, and Mackinac. The Indian nations did not understand why the British did nothing to help them. New settlers kept coming, taking as their own the traditional Indian lands, pushing the Shawnee off their northern land—the land the treaty of 1782 had promised would not be taken over.

The next year, the British and the Americans signed another treaty, the Treaty of Paris. From the Indian point of view, it was worse than the one that had gone before. Once again the British had not done anything to provide for the Indian nations and, this time, had given land to the United States that was not theirs to give. No one seemed to think or care about the Native Americans who were living on that land. The British came to regret giving away the land. They wanted the Americans to create a "neutral Indian state" made up of most or all of the territory from the Ohio River north to the Canadian boundary. But the Americans had what they wanted—the land—and they were not interested in donating any part of it to serve as a cushion between the United States and British Canada. So the Shawnee did what they had to, what their code of honor de-

In 1783 representatives from the United States and England signed the Treaty of Paris, which formally ended the American Revolution.

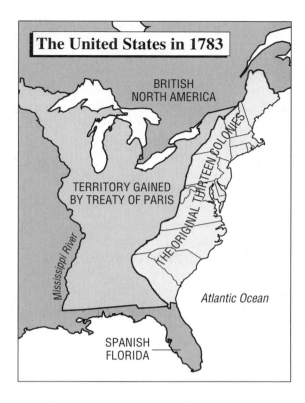

The United States in 1783

BRITISH NORTH AMERICA

TERRITORY GAINED BY TREATY OF PARIS

THE ORIGINAL THIRTEEN COLONIES

Mississippi River

Atlantic Ocean

SPANISH FLORIDA

manded—they fought to hold onto their hunting lands. The British withdrew along the Ohio, leaving the Shawnee and the white settlers to battle for land.

Honor Above All

By the time the second British-American treaty was signed, Tecumseh was fifteen years old, well on his way to becoming a man. Most Shawnee boys became men between the ages of sixteen and twenty. By then they had some skill with the Shawnee weapons of war—bows and stone-tipped arrows, stone tomahawks, and two-foot-long, wooden, long-handled war clubs with a round ball-like head, often studded with metal spikes.

In all his fifteen years Tecumseh had known nothing but war and invasion by the land-hungry people who had killed his father. Small wonder that from the time he was very young, Tecumseh had been both courageous and alert. He was a warrior and had gone along on some raids. At the age of nine and a half, some three or four years younger than was customary among the Shawnee, he had been invited to join a war party led by Chiksika. The adventure was not what Tecumseh had expected, however, and he had let fear get the better of him, deserting his party and running away from the fighting as fast as he could. It was the first and last time in his life that Tecumseh showed fear. He gave his solemn word that he would never act that way again—and he never did.

Time went by, and the conflict between the Shawnee and the Americans showed no signs of letting up. Tecumseh, now a young man of seventeen, joined a band of Shawnee who had been attacking flatboats carrying goods and settlers down the Ohio River. On one trip, rivermen on the flatboat were bringing blankets, bales of cotton, and barrels of sugar, salt, flour, gunpowder, and tea to the settlers just above the mouth of the Scioto River. The Shawnee took over the boat, killing almost everyone aboard, crew and passengers alike. Only one man survived, and he was made to suffer. The Shawnee painted him black, kept him in the village overnight, and the next day tied him with a vine to a white oak tree. A horrified Tecumseh watched as the prisoner was tortured with burning brands and burnt at the stake. Tecumseh knew that when his people won a battle, they often tortured prisoners to death. Even though he hated whites, Tecumseh found such torture wrong and could not keep silent. While the fires

The Fate of Tecumseh

Present-day historian William H. Van Hoose, the author of Tecumseh: An Indian Moses, *pictures how Tecumseh must have felt as he was growing into manhood.*

"He heard elders talk of earlier times when only Indians lived in the Northwest. Their minds were rich with memories of the past when there were no trespassers and houses and fences were not raised on the borders of the forest. Listening, Tecumseh was sometimes tempted to take a journey backward through time to the south, where his ancestors hunted in the marshes of Florida and Georgia. But his journey was in the future and it would not end until he had traveled throughout the northwest and into the south at least half a dozen times.

Now he watched a familiar scene: the men in Chillicothe preparing for another battle with the Long Knives. This had been going on for as long as he could remember. Some of those preparing to ride off to war were only a few years older than he. He was now feeling the urge to join them.

In a few years, these and many other warriors would be gone, driven into the ground in the rush to settle the Northwest. Their graves would go unmarked and their names would remain as unknown as those of the white men who killed them. He, too, would go before his time, but his name would be remembered in the history books."

burned, he spoke out strongly against this Shawnee custom. A man, he said, does not show cruelty to the helpless. He spoke with such intensity and passion that he convinced every brave there to take a vow not to torture a helpless person ever again. Prisoners might be enslaved, ransomed, or adopted, to mention three other Shawnee practices; torture was no longer acceptable.

Tecumseh had learned something too—about himself. He had powerful thoughts and he could gain a lot sharing them with others. His words, too, were powerful. Together they could be a mighty weapon, one he could use to sway people and even change the course of history. Never would he torture prisoners or make war on women and children. And never would he allow his followers to do so either.

A Final Plea for Reason

Tecumseh was not the only Native American who was learning about speaking out and about power. In 1786, the Seneca chief Sagoyewatha—"Red Jacket"—summoned delegates from many Indian nations across the country to a council at the mouth of the Detroit River. There were more than two thousand Indians present at this council, the first Tecumseh ever attended. About a year earlier some Indian leaders had tried to form a confederacy, but without much success. When Tecumseh heard this, he was amazed. This was something he had been thinking about for a long time. He was sure that the only way his people could survive the never-ending march of Americans was to band together and act as one. He listened closely as twenty-eight-year-old Red Jacket spoke. Quietly and slowly at first, Red Jacket directed his words to the Congress of the United States:

> It is now more than three years since peace was made between the King of Great Britain and you, but we . . . were disappointed, finding ourselves not included in that peace, according to our expectations. We thought that its conclusion would have promoted a friendship between the United States and Indians and we might enjoy that happiness that formerly existed between ourselves and our elder brothers, the British. . . . We have received two very agreeable messages from the thirteen United States. . . . We thought we were entering upon a reconciliation and friendship with a set of people born on the same continent with ourselves.

His voice rising with passion and anger, Red Jacket went on to say that the Indian nations had told the Americans before of their plan to bring about a "firm and lasting peace and reconciliation." He went on to explain the plan again. "The first step," he said, "should be that all treaties carried on with the United States on our part should be with the general voice of the whole Confederacy and carried on in the most open manner, without any restraint on either side. . . . [W]e hold it indispensably [absolutely] necessary that if any cessions [giving over] of our lands should be made, it should be in the most public manner and by the united voice of the Confederacy—holding all partial treaties as void and of no effect."

Red Jacket kept speaking, explaining that the Indian nations had done everything in their power to convince the Americans to follow the plan and to "promote peace and concord" between them. But nothing had happened. So Red Jacket suggested they have a treaty in the early

Seneca chief Red Jacket, shown here as an elderly man, encouraged Indian nations to unite and defend themselves against the whites.

spring and meet "on a footing of friendship." "Brothers," he said, his voice getting a hard edge to it,

we say let us meet halfway and let us pursue such steps as are becoming to upright and honest men. We beg that you will prevent your surveyors and other people coming upon our side of the Ohio River. We have told you before we wished to pursue just . . . steps, and we are determined that they shall appear just and reasonable in the eyes of the world. . . . We shall likewise prevent our people from going over. . . . It shall not be our fault if the plan we have suggested to you [is not] carried into execution. Brothers, in that case, the event will be very precarious [risky]. And, if fresh ruptures issue, we hope we will be able to [clear] ourselves—and shall, most assuredly, with our united force, should we unfortunately be obliged to defend those

rights and privileges which have been transmitted to us by our ancestors. And if we should, thereby, be reduced to misfortunes, the world will pity us when they think of the amicable proposals we now make to prevent the unnecessary [spilling] of blood. These are our thoughts and our firm resolves and we earnestly desire that you will transmit to us, as soon as possible, your answer, be it what it may.[9]

Almost everyone was impressed by the message and by the skill with which Red Jacket had given it. But Tecumseh still had doubts. He was disappointed that Red Jacket had not come up with a good plan to develop a confederacy. And he was sure that the United States did not want peace any more than it would want a confederacy. What the Americans wanted, thought Tecumseh, was to conquer all the Indian nations and make their lands part of the United States. Of what benefit, he wondered, was all this talk to the Shawnee?

"Begone! I am Tecumseh"

In The Heroes of Defeat, *William Jackson Armstrong relates this story showing that Tecumseh gained a reputation for fairness and was respected not only by his people but by whites as well.*

"[Tecumseh's] reputation for humanity, indeed, became soon widespread among the white race. Being present . . . when a band of drunken savages offered violence to the wife of a settler, he imperiously ordered them to desist. A party of white men arriving offered their protection. Pointing to Tecumseh, the woman said: 'While that man is here, I do not need protection.' On a still later occasion he rushed on a group of Indians about to do violence to a white prisoner. The Indians resisting, he said: 'Begone! I am Tecumseh.' The savages fled at the sound of the magic name."

Despite Red Jacket's attempts to form an Indian confederacy, Indian nations across the country fell to the Americans.

Nothing Changes

Tecumseh turned out to be right. In the same year as the council, Indian nations from Florida to the Great Lakes were forced by whites to migrate from their hunting grounds, and most Shawnees moved into northeastern Ohio and eastern Indiana.

Within two years the Americans secured part of Ohio by means of another treaty with Indian nations that neither lived nor hunted on lands they had given away. The Shawnee and Miami—who lived in the territory but had not signed the treaty—flatly refused to accept the transfer. As far as they were concerned, the whites were invading their land. Words had not helped. Maybe raiding would.

Tecumseh took part in many of the raids and even led some. He had become well known and respected among his people. He had been lucky so far, escaping injury during the raids. He had only one wound—from an accident during a buffalo hunt when his horse stepped into a gopher hole. Tecumseh went flying and landed on a rock, breaking his left thigh bone. He rested for a long time, waiting for the leg to heal. In time it did. But the bone was never completely straight again. The Shawnee warrior had a long curved scar on his leg, and he often walked with a limp.

The Death of a Brother

In 1787 there was a lull in the fighting, and the Shawnee built a new village of Chillicothe. Chiksika decided that this period of relative calm would be a good time to go to Tennessee to see his wife and daughter, who were staying with his wife's people, the Cherokee. This would be Tecumseh's second long trip with his older brother. The first one had occurred when he was only twelve.

Chiksika, Tecumseh, and ten of their friends set off, heading west. They planned to be gone for two or three years. They stopped and visited many Indian nations along the way: Miami, Kickapoo, and Creek as well as Shawnee and Cherokee. In April 1789 they came to their mother's Shawnee village in Missouri. They had not seen Methotasa, their mother, since she had left them in the care of their sister Tecumapese many years before. Upon arriving at the village, however, they found that their mother had gone to Tennessee, where her people, the Cherokee, now lived.

From newly built Fort Washington in Ohio (pictured), General Josiah Harmar was to lead an assault on the northwestern Indian nations. His crushing defeat ruined both his reputation and his military career.

When Tecumseh and the others finally arrived in Tennessee, they learned that here, too, whites were swallowing up Cherokee land just as they had absorbed Shawnee land. The Cherokee asked Chiksika and his party to help raid the whites. One night after Tecumseh, six other Shawnee, and seven Cherokee had made camp, they were taken by surprise by forty whites. Unafraid, Tecumseh barked commands to his companions and led them in an attack that sent the whites running. Two of the whites were killed, but not one of Tecumseh's party had so much as a scratch. The story of Tecumseh's bravery and quick thinking spread, winning him much respect among the Cherokees.

In time Tecumseh and Chiksika found the village to which their mother had gone, but the trip had been very hard on the older woman, and she had died two weeks earlier, shortly after arriving. Having found this out, Tecumseh and Chiksika went on to the village of Chiksika's wife, where they planned a long visit. During their stay, they went out on raids with the Cherokee. One night Chiksika took Tecumseh aside and told him that during their raid the next day, "when the sun is highest," he, Chiksika, would die from a bullet wound in the forehead. He also told Tecumseh to carry on for the Shawnee people and become their leader:

> You will do this, I know. I have looked ahead and seen you not only as the chief of the Shawnees, but as the greatest and most powerful leader the Indians have ever known. I have seen you journey to far lands—to where we have gone together and far beyond—and I have watched you bring together under your hand a brotherhood of Indians such as has never before been known. This I tell you. This I know to be true.[10]

The next day Chiksika died exactly as he had predicted, and Tecumseh took his brother's place as leader of their small band. Before long, Tecumseh decided that the time had come to return home.

Harmar's Defeat

While Tecumseh had been away, many more white settlers had come, and the friction between Indians and whites was at an all-time high. Over four years, thirty thousand pioneers were added to the population of the western territory. A new American fort, Fort Washington, had been built on the Ohio River, where the city of

Cincinnati, Ohio, stands today. From there, General Josiah Harmar was to lead a large force of American soldiers and state militiamen against the Indian nations in the northwest. The general had orders from President George Washington to stop the Indians from resisting. Meanwhile, the chief of the Miamis, Michikinikwa—"Little Turtle"—had asked Tecumseh to help him and the Shawnee chief Blue Jacket fight the Americans. Together they defeated Harmar and all his troops. It was a disaster for the Americans.

The Americans got even by destroying Indian villages, bushels of corn, and fruit trees, and stealing or shooting any horses they came across on their way back to Fort Washington. Tecumseh and several dozen warriors kept a watch on them all the way, sniping at them every chance they got. By the time Harmar reached Fort Washington, he had lost several hundred men, another fifty or so had been wounded, and the rest were exhausted and hungry. The episode ruined Harmar's reputation and ended his army career.

The Ordinance of 1787

The Ordinance of 1787, which established the Northwest Territory, stated that the land was to be divided into no less than three or no more than five states. Kentuckians had a strong reaction to the following part of the ordinance, quoted in The Frontiersmen.

"The utmost faith shall always be observed towards the Indians; their lands and property shall never be taken from them without their consent; and in their property, rights, and liberty they shall never be invaded or disturbed, unless in just and lawful wars authorized by Congress; but laws founded in justice and humanity shall, from time to time, be made, for preventing wrongs being done to them, and for preserving peace and friendship with them."

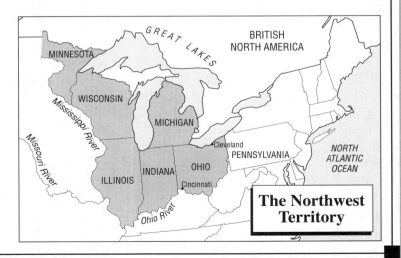

The Northwest Territory

3 Uniting a People

Tecumseh turned twenty-three in 1791. By then, his name and his reputation as a brave warrior, strong leader, and forceful speaker had spread across the southeastern states. He had been fighting the Long Knives for a long time. When would it end? When would they stop coming? Although Tecumseh knew whites outnumbered his people, he did not know how vastly.

The Defeat of St. Clair

Now the Indians faced yet a new enemy— General Arthur St. Clair, governor of the Northwest Territory. Determined to drive the Indians out, St. Clair set off with a force of Long Knives for the Wabash River in the autumn of 1791. St. Clair had been a hero during the American Revolution, but he did not know anything about fighting Indians. To make matters worse, sometimes his gout, a painful disease of the joints, was so bad that he had to be carried on a litter. The campaign St. Clair led was described by a nineteenth-century American woman whose interest in Tecumseh led her to write a book about him:

> The young warrior Tecumseh was sent out with a party of spies to watch the movements of this new expedition. St.

Clair, a brave and veteran soldier, began his march cautiously at the head of fourteen hundred troops. Two forts were erected about forty miles apart, on the route, for places of deposit, and to secure safety in case of retreat. While Tecumseh and his party were lying on Nettle Creek, a stream which

General Arthur St. Clair, governor of the Northwest Territory, boldly set out to eliminate the Indians, only to discover his forces were no match for the clever warriors.

Tecumseh, the Warrior

In 1899, more than eighty-five years after Tecumseh's death, historian Warren King Moorehead published a paper about the Indian nations of Ohio. Here he pays tribute to Tecumseh and explains why the Shawnee leader was a great warrior.

"And now we come to the greatest aborigine of the Ohio Valley, a man . . . who certainly ranked not lower than second in the long list of celebrities of the American race. I refer to Tecumtha, or Tkamthi, popularly called Tecumseh. . . . [H]e was but a youth during the period of the Revolution, yet his boyhood days were spent among scenes of activity—the coming and going of innumerable war parties, the attacks of soldiers upon his people's villages. Reared among such surroundings, hearing the beat of the war-drum from earliest infancy, it is no wonder that he imbibed the military spirit and . . . 'liked the music of the harp, and the organ still better, but he liked the fife and drum best of all because they made his heart beat quick.'

. . . There is no instance during his entire lifetime of his preserving other than a defiant attitude toward whites. Strong in his self-reliance born of an intrepid nature, he was a moving and controlling spirit among all the tribes of the northwest. Possessing much personal magnetism he drew around him all the dissatisfied Indians. These were of all tongues and conditions, yet he molded the whole into an effective and well-drilled army and one which was more frequently victorious than overcome."

flows into the Great Miami, St. Clair passed out through Greenville to the head waters of the Wabash.

On the morning after St. Clair reached the high ground on the upper Wabash, the writer continued, his inexperience with Indian-style warfare caught up with him:

General St. Clair, who had no skill in Indian warfare, was suddenly, at a moment when he fancied himself secure, attacked on all sides by an overwhelming force of Indians, who had long been hanging upon his flanks, and had thus become thoroughly acquainted with the numbers and disposition of his troops. The soldiers fought bravely, but seeing themselves environed [surrounded] on all sides by countless hordes of savages, they became panic-stricken and fled, pursued by the Indians, who filled the air with demoniac yells.[11]

For the Americans, it was one of the worst defeats ever. For the Indians, it was the greatest victory over any American military force ever. More than nine hundred U.S. officers and men had taken part in the battle. Only two dozen came back uninjured. St. Clair was one of the few who escaped alive. Indian casualties were fewer: sixty-six warriors lost and only nine wounded.

A Worthy Enemy

For a while, the flood of whites slowed a little. The Indians had gotten back some of their confidence. They also had enough spoils from St. Clair's troops and their followers to see them through the winter. But

Tecumseh knew that neither the calm nor the supply of goods would last forever. So he kept on making trouble for any white who dared to settle on his land.

In 1792, on the way back from a series of successful raids, Tecumseh and his band went on a horse-stealing outing in Kentucky. They took their first twenty-one horses from a large fenced lot easily enough. They caught the horses by feeding them bits of maple sugar, then blindfolded them with strips of cloth, tied a rope to each, and calmly and silently led the little herd away. At the next stop, they repeated the routine. This time they got more than thirty horses. Finally they stopped and set up camp. About midnight, one of the braves threw some more wood on the fire to keep it going. It cost him his life, for it drew gunfire from a

After stealing horses from a wagon train, braves stay out of sight by clinging to the steeds. Raids on white settlements provided Indians with a valuable supply of goods and horses and also discouraged many Americans from settling on Indian lands.

band of whites led by a famous frontiersman named Simon Kenton. Hearing gunshots, Tecumseh came running out of his tent screaming at the others to attack. As Tecumseh's war club crushed the skull of one of the raiders, Kenton urged his followers to run away fast.

A few years later, a writer described what happened.

> The whole skirmish lasted but a few minutes. Just as the retreat was commenced, John Barr . . . was killed, and Alexander McIntire was taken prisoner, and the next day killed. The residue of Kenton's little band arrived in safety at home. . . . The celebrated Tecumseh commanded the Indians. His caution and fearless intrepidity [bravery] made him a host [the equivalent of a great many men] wherever he went. In military tactics, night attacks are not allowable, except in cases like this. . . . Sometimes in night attacks, panics and confusion are created in the attacked party which may render them a prey to inferior numbers. Kenton trusted to something like this . . . , but was disappointed; for where Tecumseh was present, his influence over the minds of his followers, infused that confidence in his tact [tactic] . . . , that they could only be defeated by force of numbers.[12]

The Time In Between

Many of the Indians thought that the white settlers would not try to make war on them anymore. But Tecumseh, Blue Jacket, and the Miami chief Little Turtle

Frontiersman Simon Kenton (pictured) and his band of men witnessed Tecumseh's bravery and influence firsthand. Tecumseh's warriors quickly defeated the white raiders, sending Kenton and the other survivors fleeing for their lives.

did not agree. They knew that it was only a matter of time until the Americans struck again. They had heard through the British that the American president had named a new commander—Major General Anthony Wayne, called "Mad Anthony" by most Americans and "Black Snake" (because he moved so slowly) by Native Americans. George Hammond, the British minister to the United States, thought Wayne was "unquestionably the most active, vigilant, and enterprising Officer in the American Service" and that he would do anything to erase the "Stain which the late defeat has cast upon American Arms."[13]

General Anthony Wayne was determined to restore the pride of the U.S. military after it had been trampled by the Indians. Shortly after he was put in command, Wayne went on a rampage building U.S. forts and destroying Native American settlements.

Wayne started drilling a special force of several thousand troops in 1792. The next year the government tried to talk peace to some Indian chiefs at a conference in Sandusky, Ohio. The chiefs, though, would not agree to anything unless the whites recognized the Ohio River as their eastern boundary. So Wayne and his troops set out. Along their way, they stopped and built two new forts—Fort Greenville and Fort Recovery.

Tecumseh, Blue Jacket, and Little Turtle began planning an attack on Fort Recovery. Little Turtle, though, was not sure that this was the right thing to do. Some of the other chiefs said that Little Turtle was too old—and too afraid—to fight. Nineteenth-century writer Elizabeth Seelye remembered his response:

We have beaten the enemy twice under different commanders. We cannot always expect the same good fortune to attend us. The Americans are now led by a chief who never sleeps. The day and night are alike to him; and during all the time he has been marching upon our villages, notwithstanding the watchfulness of our young men, we have been unable to surprise him. Think well of it. There is something that whispers to me that it would be prudent to listen to his offers of peace.[14]

While Wayne moved ahead, stopping along the way to build bridges and forts, Miamis, Shawnees, Ottawas, Potawatomis, Wyandots, Chippewas, and others headed toward Fort Recovery. Wayne was still at Greenville in mid-1794 when they arrived at the fort, so they split into two bands. While one tried to attack the fort, the other tried to steal the three hundred packhorses the Long Knives were moving from the fort to Greenville. Both attempts failed, and some of the braves started arguing among themselves. Angry and frustrated, many of the warriors departed, leaving only six hundred to go up against Wayne's four thousand troops.

The Battle of Fallen Timbers

On August 20, 1794, Wayne and his troops attacked the warriors at a place called Fallen Timbers, so named because a heavy thunderstorm had left the ground along the northwest bank of the Maumee River littered with broken trees and branches. By that time, many more warriors had shown up, bringing their number up to about two thousand.

The fighting was fierce, and Tecumseh's party of scouts, who met the first charge of the infantry, got the worst of it. One of Tecumseh's younger brothers was among the first to fall—shot through the head. The chiefs knew that courage alone could not stop the Long Knives from overwhelming and defeating them. So Blue Jacket called for a retreat to a British fort about three miles away. The British had promised to help the Indians.

At the fort, the tired and discouraged warriors received yet another nasty surprise. The British soldiers refused to come

The Shame of St. Clair

As George Washington's comments to his private secretary, quoted by Allan Eckert in his biography of Tecumseh, clearly show, the president was furious with General St. Clair for the horrible defeat in 1791.

"Right here, yes, on this very spot, I took leave of him. I wished him success and honor. 'You have your instructions,' I said, 'from the Secretary of War. I had a strict eye to them [reviewed them carefully] and will add but one word—beware of a surprise!'—I repeated it—'BEWARE OF A SURPRISE! You know how the Indians fight us!' He went off with that, as my last solemn warning thrown into his ears. And yet!—to suffer that army to be cut to pieces, hacked, butchered, tomahawked, by a surprise—the very thing I guarded him against! Oh, God! Oh, God, he is worse than a murderer! How can he answer to it to his country? The blood of the slain is upon him—the curse of widows and orphans—the curse of Heaven!"

out and help them. And, even worse, no matter how hard the Indians pounded on the gates, the British refused to admit their former allies. The gates remained closed and locked. Tecumseh and Blue Jacket were furious. Finally Blue Jacket gave the order for the warriors to make a run for it. Tecumseh stewed—the British had insulted them. That was something he would remember for a long time.

Meanwhile, Wayne marched his men through one Indian village after another, leveling each one to the ground. The soldiers burned storehouses and cornfields, leaving the people who had lived in the villages without a supply of food to see them through winter. Kinjoino, an Ottawa chief who had fought at the Battle of Fallen Timbers, claimed that the defeat had oc-curred because "the Great Spirit was angry and She turned Her face away from Her red children."[15] He was not the only one who believed that. The Indian nations now had to admit to themselves that they were not the controlling force in their country—the Americans were.

The Treaty of Greenville

One after another, Native Americans went to see General Wayne. They wanted peace, they told him—at just about any price. Prisoners were exchanged. Even whites like Sinnantha, who had been adopted into an Indian nation, who had been much loved by their adopted people, and

An Indian warrior fires upon the charging Americans during the bloody Battle of Fallen Timbers.

American general Anthony Wayne (right) proved to be an adept opponent for the Native Americans. After Wayne's victory at the Battle of Fallen Timbers, representatives from numerous Indian nations flocked to the general, each hoping to make peace.

who had fought with them against the whites, were returned.

Tecumseh was not one who wanted Wayne's favors. He kept on speaking out against any kind of peace treaty with the Americans. Blue Jacket, who had been like a brother to Tecumseh, had gone along with the others in their desire for peace. But even he could not make Tecumseh change his mind. Tecumseh took a small group of followers and set up a village at Deer Creek. There, he said, they would wait to see what happened.

In July 1795 more than a thousand Indians representing twelve different Indian nations—Wyandot, Shawnee, Miami, Delaware, Ottawa, Chippewa, Potawatomi, Kickapoo, Kaskaskia, Wea, the Eel River Miami, and Piankeshaw—met at Greenville, Ohio, with General Wayne and others, including twenty-two-year-old William Henry Harrison, the new commander of Fort Washington. The Fox and Sac had been invited but had refused to come. Some ninety chiefs signed the Treaty of Greenville, which gave the

No Compromise

In 1793 the United States agreed to abandon its forts inside Indian boundaries and give the Indian nations supplies and $50,000 if the Indians would admit that the U.S. government had some rights on the lands north of the Ohio River. As the following speech, quoted in The Heroes of Defeat, *shows, the Indian nations refused the offer.*

"Money to us is of no value and to most of us unknown. No consideration whatever can induce us to sell the lands on which we get sustenance for our women and children. . . . We know that these settlers are poor, or they would never have ventured to live in a country which has been in continual trouble ever since they crossed the Ohio. Divide . . . this large sum of money which you have offered us among those people. . . . We maintain that the King of England . . . never had a right to give you our country. . . .

You have talked to us about concessions. It appears strange that you should expect any from us who have only been defending our just rights against your invasions. You make one concession by offering us money and another by agreeing to do us justice after having long . . . withheld it. Brothers, we shall be persuaded that you mean to do us justice if you agree that the Ohio shall remain the boundary between us. We want peace. . . .

Restore to us our country and we shall be enemies no longer. We desire you to consider that our only demand is the peaceable possession of a small part of our once great country. Look back and review the lands from whence we have been driven to this spot. We can retreat no further, because the country behind hardly affords food for its present inhabitants. We have therefore resolved to leave our bones in this small space to which we are now confined. This is our answer. Go tell Washington!"

whites most of Ohio, part of Indiana, and such other areas as Detroit. Within the boundaries signed over to the United States were twenty-five thousand square miles of land that had been home to the Shawnee.

The chiefs had signed away their hunting grounds, given the United States sixteen tracts of land within their territory for government reservations and sole rights to make treaties for their lands, and agreed not to protest invasion by whites into the Ohio Valley. What did the nations that signed the treaty get in return? A little less than $2,500 worth of goods each—about one cent for every six acres. But the

Indian nations were pleased. They wanted peace. Said one Wyandot chief, "We . . . acknowledge the fifteen United States . . . to be our father . . . (and) must call them brother no more."[16]

Tecumseh stayed in his village. He wanted no part of the council or the treaty. He thought the chiefs who had signed it were fools. Tecumseh never—not before or after—signed any treaty with the United States. Blue Jacket and several of his other friends came to tell Tecumseh the terms of the treaty. As they were leaving, the Shawnee voiced his sadness and spoke of the dream that was to consume him for the rest of his life:

> My heart is a stone, heavy with sadness for my people; cold with the knowledge that no treaty will keep the whites out of our lands; hard with the determination to resist as long as I live and breathe. Now we are weak and many of our people are afraid. But hear me: a

single twig breaks, but the bundle of twigs is strong. Someday I will embrace our brother tribes and draw them into a bundle and together we will win our country back from the whites.[17]

Tecumseh spoke out against the treaty, the terms of which he knew by heart, at every chance. He had to make his people understand. Didn't they realize that the treaty would open the Northwest and bring more white settlers than ever before? If all the Indian nations stood strong together, they could stop the Long Knives from taking what little they had left. And they could take back much of what they had lost. This became Tecumseh's vision—a united nation of Native Americans stretching across the land from the Great Lakes to the Gulf of Mexico. In the next century, speaking of another set of issues, an American statesman summed up Tecumseh's philosophy, the message he spent his life trying to get across to his

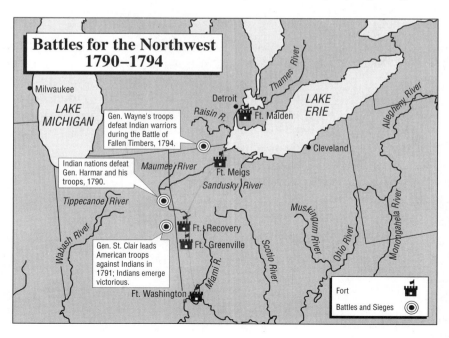

Battles for the Northwest 1790–1794

Gen. Wayne's troops defeat Indian warriors during the Battle of Fallen Timbers, 1794.

Indian nations defeat Gen. Harmar and his troops, 1790.

Gen. St. Clair leads American troops against Indians in 1791; Indians emerge victorious.

Fort

Battles and Sieges

In July 1795, Indian chiefs met with U.S. officials for the signing of the Treaty of Greenville (pictured). The agreement, which had excluded Shawnee representatives, gave Americans land in Ohio, Indiana, and Illinois, as well as twenty-five thousand miles of Shawnee territory.

people—united we stand, divided we fall. If Tecumseh could bring all the nations together into one, the United States would become no more than a narrow strip along the Atlantic coast.

When the Delawares who lived on the south shore of the White River in present-day Indiana invited Tecumseh and his followers to live with them, he accepted. He settled his people just west of the Greenville treaty line on the banks of the Wabash River. He fully agreed with the Shawnee chief Kekewepellethe, who in 1786 had told the Americans, "God gave us this country. We do not understand measuring out the lands; it is all ours."[18] For close to twenty years, Tecumseh used his strength and power to keep alive the question of who truly owned much of the land of the United States.

Chapter

4 Family Ties

By 1797 some important changes had taken place. John Adams was now president of the United States. And what Tecumseh had been saying all along was beginning to be heard—and understood—by the people of the Indian nations of the Northwest Territory. Not long before Tecumseh had gotten married, his life and hopes and those of his younger brother Lowawluwaysica began to come together.

The Marriages of Tecumseh

While he was living in the village of Deer Creek, Tecumseh caught the eye of twenty-three-year-old Mohnetohse, the daughter of a Peckuwe Shawnee warrior who lived in the village. She made up her mind to marry the young Shawnee. The couple were married in 1796, and their son Mahyawwekawpawe was born the same year. When the baby was almost two months old, Tecumseh said he never wanted to see Mohnetohse again and sent her back to her parents. He gave his baby son to his sister Tecumapese to raise.

Very soon Tecumseh married again. He wanted a mother for his son, someone who would care for his needs and give him more children. His new wife, whose name was Mamate, became ill and died in 1797, right after the birth of their son Naythawaynah—"A Panther Seizing Its Prey." Now Tecumapese had two nephews to raise. Around the same time, Tecumseh visited a white friend, a settler named James Galloway. Galloway had a young

In the span of two years, Tecumseh had been married twice and fathered two sons. After the marriages ended, Tecumseh gave his children to his sister Tecumapese to rear.

daughter, Rebecca, a gentle, laughing, blue-eyed blonde, called "Star of the Lake" by Tecumseh. When Rebecca grew older, she told everyone that she and Tecumseh had been in love and that he had asked her to marry him. The marriage never took place, she said, because she could not live happily in the Shawnee world and Tecumseh would not agree to live among the whites. She had made up the story of the romance and repeated it so many times that people came to believe it. Her brother even wrote about it. By then it is likely that Rebecca herself believed it.

Lowawluwaysica

Tecumseh's brother Lowawluwaysica—"He Makes a Loud Noise"—was only three years younger than Tecumseh, one of the triplets. Lowawluwaysica got his name because when he was a baby he cried a lot for no reason. Lowawluwaysica adored Tecumseh, following him around whenever and wherever he could. But as Lowawluwaysica began to grow older, along with love for his brother came envy. Tecumseh was good-looking, well liked, and did everything well. The younger boy, on the other hand, was not at all attractive physically and was not liked. He was intelligent but was not the best at anything.

A clumsy child, Lowawluwaysica had shown no talent for games or for hunting. Tecumseh tried to teach him to be a good hunter, but without much success. One day when Lowawluwaysica was ten or eleven years old, he went with Tecumseh and some other young boys Tecumseh was teaching to hunt. One of the boys shot at

Although Lowawluwaysica tried to follow in the footsteps of his great brother, he had difficulty providing for his family and was considered an outcast by his community.

a bird in flight and missed. As the arrow returned to earth, everyone ducked—except Lowawluwaysica. He looked up to see the falling arrow. His screams of pain pierced the air as he collapsed, the barbed flint arrowhead sticking out of his right eye. Tecumseh pulled out the arrowhead, but the eye could not be saved.

Even as a child, Lowawluwaysica had no real friends. He had a bad temper, almost always wore a frown, was rude, and had little sense of humor. Even Chiksika and Tecumapese had ignored him most of the time. As he grew older, Lowawluwaysica did just about anything he could to get attention. He talked loudly. He boasted. He picked fights. At the Battle of

Fallen Timbers, however, he vanished when the battle was at its worst and hid away for several days.

In time Lowawluwaysica married and had children of his own. But he couldn't provide enough game to feed his family. What meat his wife and children had came from Tecumseh, and he was the one who repaired the family's *wigewa*, or home. It was only because of their liking and respect for Tecumseh that the other villagers put up with Lowawluwaysica at all.

Lowawluwaysica was twenty-four years old when Tecumseh announced his opposition to the Greenville treaty. He stood behind his older brother and went with him to Deer Creek, where an old Shawnee medicine man and prophet named Penegashega—"Change of Feathers"—began to train him in traditional medicine. Soon Lowawluwaysica started visiting the sick and thinking of himself as the village doctor. He sang the healing chants he had learned from Change of Feathers and carried his own medicine pouch filled with herbs, bits of bone, and secret items.

Lowawluwaysica, though, had a problem—really, an illness. He liked the white man's whiskey, which he had been drinking since he was nine or ten years old. Often firewater was the payment he asked for making someone well. He was not the only Native American to become addicted to whiskey. White traders trying to strike a bargain with the Indian nations often bid for trade by offering generous amounts of whiskey. Tecumseh spoke out against the practice, but his brother was one of many who had not listened.

While conducting business with Indians, white traders often enticed potential customers with whiskey. Lowawluwaysica, like many other Native Americans, became addicted to the Americans' firewater.

Two Prominent Men

Thomas L. McKenney, a member of the federal Indian Department in the 1800s, offered this view of Tecumseh and his brother the Prophet, in the history book he wrote with James Hall.

"The Indiana territory having been recently organized, and Governor Harrison being invested with the office of superintendent of Indian affairs, it became his duty to hold frequent treaties [meetings] with the Indians; and, on these occasions, Tecumthé and the Prophet were prominent men. The latter is described as the most graceful and agreeable of Indian orators; he was easy, subtle, and insinuating—not powerful, but persuasive in argument; and it was remarked, that he never spoke when Tecumthé was present. He was the instrument, and Tecumthé the master-spirit, the bold warrior, the able, eloquent, fearless speaker, who, in any assembly of his own race, awed all around him by the energy of his character, and stood forward as the leading individual."

When Lowawluwaysica was thirty years old, he was described as follows:

Not really thin, yet his features were hatchetlike, with the nose sharply beaked, the cheekbones relatively high and the cheeks themselves hollow. One of his ears had a lobe half again as long as the other and when he smiled, his thin lips crooked up on the right but down on the left. Over his empty eyesocket he had recently begun wearing a black eye patch. . . . In character he remained as he had always been— high-strung, nervous, and unusually irritable. His rare, explosive laughter . . . was a shrill and grating cackle with a witchlike quality. He was swift to accuse unjustifiably, swift to take offense at imagined slights, and very susceptible to bursts of blind rage.[19]

Will of the Brothers

In August 1805, in the Ohio Shawnee village of Tara, the old medicine man Change of Feathers died. This was the opening Tecumseh and Lowawluwaysica had been waiting for.

Tecumseh told his brother to gather together everyone in the village and say that he, Lowawluwaysica, had had a vision in which he had seen three sick villagers die. Then, said Tecumseh, he was to announce that he, Lowawluwaysica, was going to cast the sickness from all the other ill villagers, who would start to get better within five days. Next he was to explain that the three who had died had practiced witchcraft and were not worthy of being saved. Last, Tecumseh told his brother to tell the people that after they have seen the prophecy come true, they were to spread word of what had happened among all Shawnee and invite everyone to come on the day following the next full moon to Tecumseh's village at Greenville to hear a very important message.

Lowawluwaysica did as he was told. He was not surprised when the prophecy Tecumseh had told him to make his own came true. The excited villagers passed on the news. Word soon spread among many villages, just as Tecumseh had known it would.

Tenskwatawa, the Prophet

On the day following the full moon, Lowawluwaysica stood on an empty wagon in Tecumseh's village at Greenville. In a circle around him, waiting to hear the important message they had been promised, were almost a thousand people. Not all were Shawnee. People from some other Indian nations had come too. So had some curious whites.

Speaking in a strong and clear voice, which kept growing in intensity and passion, Lowawluwaysica talked for more than three hours. From this time on, he announced, he would be known as Tenskwatawa—"One with Open Mouth," or "Open Door." Change of Feathers was dead, he reminded them, and he wanted to be the new Shawnee prophet. He could be the open door through which God spoke to them, through which they would enter a happier, holier life. Would the people let him be their prophet? Their answer was yes.

As Tenskwatawa, the Prophet, Lowawluwaysica gained fame among his people. Tenskwatawa did not possess the gift of prophecy, however, and had to rely on Tecumseh for his inspiration.

Tenskwatawa told how the Great Spirit had taken him up into the clouds on the day that Change of Feathers died. The very first thing Tenskwatawa had seen were the people who had died from drinking the white man's whiskey. All of them were suffering, he said, with flames of fire coming from their mouths in a never-ending stream. It had scared him so, he told them, that he had made himself a promise. Never again would he drink—and they must not either. Whiskey, he warned, was poison. It was cursed. He had seen the suffering of those who had died of it.

Tenskwatawa went on to talk of how Indians should give up the ways of the white man and return to the traditions of their ancestors, to the ways they had followed before the whites and their descendants had come to their lands. Eat corn and wild game, he told them, not the soft white bread of the Long Knives. Hunt with bow and arrow, and share your game with one another. Use the rifle only for self-defense. "You must not dress like the White Man or wear hats like them," he continued. "And when the weather is not severe, you must go naked excepting the Breach cloth, and when you are clothed,

Indians trade with Americans in a frontier town. The Prophet preached against such contact. Instead, he asked Native Americans to return to their traditional lifestyles.

The "Open Door"

The Prophet made an impression on many of his people. But, as Jacob P. Dunn shows in True Indian Stories, *not everyone was influenced.*

"[The Prophet] said the 'Great Spirit told him to go and warn his people of danger and call upon them to put away their sins and be good. Whereupon he began to speak to them in great distress, he would weep and tremble while addressing them. Some believed, were greatly alarmed, began to confess their sins, forsake them, and set out to be good. . . . But some were very wicked and tried to keep the people from believing, and encouraged them in their former wicked ways.'"

it must be in skins or leather of your own Dressing."[20]

Above all, Tenskwatawa preached, Indian women had to stop marrying whites. The races were separate and distinct—and had to stay that way. Even though legend did not say so, the Great Spirit who had created the Shawnee had not created the whites. Whites were the children of the Evil Spirit, who had created them to lead Native Americans astray. The best thing any Indian could do, Tenskwatawa declared, was to stay away from whites entirely.

Tenskwatawa told his listeners to stop quarreling and warring among themselves. Other Indian nations, he insisted, were not the enemy. They needed to live in peace with their neighbors, to be just and kind, to pay their debts, and to tell the truth. They also must respect their elders and must own all property in common. The Indian, he declared, was superior to any other race, especially to the whites. His brother Tecumseh, he proclaimed, would lead them to glory.

Standing there on the wagon, the new prophet announced that the Great Spirit had given him magic powers. He had already shown once, had he not, that he could predict the future? Had he not already shown, too, how he could heal the sick? He had the power to cheat death both in sickness and on the battlefield. He promised his people that when they lived according to the way he had preached, the Great Spirit would reward them. They would be happy again—as they had been before the whites came. The white race would be destroyed, proclaimed the Prophet, and the North American Indians would get their land back just as it had been in the past before the Long Knives came.

Toward the end of his speech Tenskwatawa invited all Indians to come to live at his brother Tecumseh's village at Greenville. It was not, he explained, a Shawnee village. It was an Indian village. All were welcome. A nineteenth-century writer, Henry Onderdonk Jr., described Tenskwatawa's exaggerations as follows:

The Medicine of Tenskwatawa

Tenskwatawa had many medicines. One of the most outstanding was described in 1830 by an artist named George Catlin. His description is quoted in Jason Hook's book Tecumseh: Visionary Chief of the Shawnee.

"He carried with him into every wig-wam that he visited, the image of a dead person of the size of life; which was made . . . of some light material, and always kept concealed under bandages of thin white muslin cloths and not to be opened; of this he made great mystery, and got his recruits to swear by touching a sacred string of white beans, which he had attached to his neck or some other way secreted about him. In this way, by his extraordinary cunning, he had carried terror into the country as far as he went; and actually enlisted some eight or ten thousand men, who were sworn to follow him home."

Artist George Catlin, who won acclaim for his paintings of Native American life, captured the mystery of the Prophet in this 1830 portrait.

The Prophet made many predictions concerning the future glory of the Indians. His disciples spread the most absurd tales about his wonderful power—that he could make pumpkins spring out of the ground as large as wigwams, and that his corn grew so large that one ear would feed a dozen men. They spread a belief that the body of the Prophet was invulnerable [could not be harmed], and that he had all knowledge, past, present, and future. It is said that so great a number flocked to Greenville to see him, that the southern shores of Lake Superior and Michigan were quite depopulated. The traders were obliged to abandon their business.[21]

The Power Behind the Prophet

Tecumseh knew better than anyone that Tenskwatawa was no prophet and had no real magic. But it did not matter. To have the others think he did served Tecumseh's purposes. With his guidance, Tenskwatawa would draw to him people of many different Indian nations.

One night, at least four years earlier, Tecumseh had told his siblings and a few close friends of his plan to unite their people and form a new village. It would not be a village of just one or a few Indian nations. It would be a village in which all thought of themselves as one race—Indian—not as Shawnee or Miami or Ottawa or any other group. He did not dream, he told them, of a confederacy like the alliances that had been tried before. His dream was broader. What he wanted was a single united Indian nation, strong enough to protect its lands and ways of life against anyone who might try to possess or change them. Ten, twelve, or more years might be needed for the dream to come true, but Tecumseh was young and patient. The same night he gave each of those with him the role he or she would have to play in realizing his dream. Lowawluwaysica, he said, must use his talent to excite people, to provoke them and make them angry. He had to make them direct that anger at the Long Knives.

Tecumseh knew what he was doing. He could not bring together all the nations by himself, no matter how long and hard he talked. On the other hand, Lowawluwaysica alone could not keep content any followers he might get. They needed each other. Pucksinwah and two of his sons—Chiksika and Tecumseh—had received the gift of prophecy, but Lowawluwaysica had not. Even as Tenskwatawa, the Shawnee prophet, he would have failed without the support of Tecumseh. He could attract followers, but he could not run a village. He had no idea how to make sure there was enough food or housing for everyone. He did not know, either, what to do if illness or disease struck the villagers. But together the two brothers—one a statesman and the other a spiritual leader—could fulfill Tecumseh's dream.

At first the power—and then, in time, the control—was in Tecumseh's hands. The Prophet, who really spoke for Tecumseh, would soon become merely a figurehead. The idea of the separation of Indians from the whites, and the prophecies Tenskwatawa would make—these were things Tecumseh had been thinking

Shaking Hands with the Prophet

A person who wanted to become a follower of the Prophet had to swear allegiance to him in a special ceremony. After confessing his sins, the follower was brought into a lodge that held some holy items. A captive named John Tanner wrote a book about his adventures, which is quoted in Tecumseh: Fact and Fiction in Early Records, *edited by Carl Frederick Klinck. This excerpt describes the secret ceremony.*

"When the people, and I among them, were brought into the long lodge, prepared for this solemnity, we saw something carefully concealed under a blanket, in figure and dimensions bearing some resemblance to the form of a man. This was accompanied by two young men, who, it was understood, attended constantly upon it, made its bed at night, as if for a man, and slept near it. But while we remained, no one went near it, or raised the blanket which was spread over its unknown contents. Four strings of mouldy and discolored beans were all the remaining visible insignia of this important mission. After a long harangue [tiresome speech] . . . , the four strings of beans, which we were told were made of the flesh itself of the prophet, were carried . . . to each man in the lodge, and he was expected to take hold of each string at the top, and draw them gently through his hand. This was called shaking hands with the prophet, and was considered as solemnly engaging to obey his injunctions [commands], and accept his mission as from the Supreme. . . .

We had already been for some time assembled in considerable numbers; much agitation and terror had prevailed among us, and now famine began to be felt. The faces of men wore an aspect of unusual gloominess: the active became indolent [lazy], and the spirits of the bravest seemed to be subdued."

about since the defeat at Fallen Timbers and the signing of the Greenville treaty. Over time, the Prophet would travel far and wide seeking new followers for his religion and new warriors for Tecumseh's war against the whites. He would cause harm to some and hurt to many, including himself and his family.

5 This Land Is Ours

While Tecumseh and the Prophet were putting their plans into action, the federal government was selling the land on which Indians had lived to settlers for two dollars an acre. So the whites kept coming, pushing the Shawnee farther and farther west and turning hunting grounds into towns. Time was running out for the Indians in the Northwest Territory.

Harrison's Concerns

The new territory of Indiana had been formed in 1800, and the first territorial governor, the youthful William Henry Harrison, was no stranger to the area or to the Shawnee. The former commander of Fort Washington had been named secretary of the Northwest Territory in 1798, had fought in the Battle of Fallen Timbers, and had been at Greenville when the treaty was signed.

As soon as Harrison became governor, Indian chiefs had started calling his attention to mistreatment of their people. Whites, the chiefs said, were killing them and their game, making their young men drunk, and cheating them. Several years after becoming governor, in a letter to Henry Dearborn, who was secretary of war under Thomas Jefferson, Harrison wrote, "I wish I could say the Indians were treated with justice and propriety on all occasions by our citizens; but it is far otherwise. They are often abused and maltreated, and it is very rare that they obtain satisfaction for the most unprovoked wrongs."[22]

William Henry Harrison, the first governor of the Indiana Territory, was extremely familiar with the Native Americans in the region. Prior to his governorship, Harrison had served as the commander of Fort Washington and had fought in the Battle of Fallen Timbers.

But knowing this did not change things. Greenville soon became the center of Harrison's attention. The more followers of the Prophet arrived there, the more nervous Harrison became. Certain that the Prophet was trying to stir up things between Indians and whites, Harrison seemed not to realize that Greenville was in Ohio, where he had no authority.

Death in Chillicothe

Early in 1803, Ohio became a state and Chillicothe its capital. When, a few months later, a white settler was found murdered not too many miles from Chillicothe, whites who blamed Indians killed an old Shawnee. Alarmed by the turn of events and fearing for their safety in the wake of the revenge killing, whites in and around Chillicothe sought help from the new governor of Ohio, Dr. Edward Tiffin. There are many Indians at Greenville, the Ohioans told Tiffin. What are they all doing there? What do they want? How will they pay back the death of the old Shawnee?

Tiffin acted quickly, calling on Tecumseh to help ease the fears of the whites. In response, Tecumseh set out immediately for Chillicothe to tell the whites that his people had not killed the settler and that the Ohioans had nothing to fear. Huge crowds gathered to listen to him speak. Among the crowd was John McDonald, the colonel of the newly formed Ohio militia, who was more than a little impressed by Tecumseh and the way he handled himself:

When Tecumseh arose to speak, he cast his gaze over the vast multitude which the interesting occasion had brought together. He appeared one of the most dignified men I have ever beheld. While this orator of nature was speaking, the immense crowd preserved the utmost silence. From the confident manner in which he spoke of the intentions of the Indians to abide by the treaty of Greenville and live in peace with their white brethren, he dispelled, as if by magic, the apprehensions of the whites. The settlers returned to their deserted farms, and business generally was resumed throughout the region.[23]

Right after the speech in Chillicothe, Tecumseh began a series of journeys to talk to members of other Indian nations near and far. His message was the same to all—as long as they remained divided, they could not defeat the Long Knives and would continue to lose their land. He was a passionate and persuasive speaker, and his reputation grew. An extremely intelligent man, he was more interested in ideas than in what he or others owned. He lived by a strict code and had a highly developed sense of justice. In a vision from his guardian spirit, the Buffalo, Tecumseh learned the sacred Buffalo Dance, which would summon the strength of the buffalo. Shawnees and Delawares, buffalo-head designs on their chests and a red line running from the outer corner of each eye, still perform this ceremonial dance.

Tecumseh was so well thought of that to him fell a major responsibility and honor. He became holder of the Kispokotha's treasured sacred bundle. In this bundle, which was opened for Shawnee war ceremonies, were four plumes of hawk feathers, a wooden image of a man in Shawnee clothing holding a tiny bow and arrows, two turkey-feather headdresses, and, according to legend, the flesh and bones of a Shawnee god—the Giant Horned Snake. Along with these items Tecumseh carried his own magic charm—an ancient steel tomahawk. His "medicine" was powerful indeed. Many years later, when asked about Tecumseh, a Winnebago who had known him remembered "a powerful man"—who could not be penetrated by bullets. "Indeed, it was impossible to kill him in any way."[24]

By 1806, even though some major chiefs of the Northwest Territory had not yet given him their full support, Tecumseh had more Indian nations pledged to him than any other union the Indian groups had ever known—or would know to this day. Tecumseh had wanted to keep the union's numbers a secret, but in March, when he met in a war council with about a thousand warriors, word got out. Afraid that there would be an uprising, the whites hurried to alert Dr. Tiffin. The governor in turn sent a messenger to the principal chiefs of the Shawnee with a letter citing the fears of the whites and requesting his "Red brethren" to "expressly state" if they "have any cause of complaint against our people." He invited them to

Indian braves wear buffalo headdresses while performing the sacred Buffalo Dance. Tecumseh's guardian spirit taught him the ceremonial dance, which was believed to summon the strength of the mighty buffalo.

tell him of any such complaint and stated that if in fact no problem existed, he could prevent any serious consequences that might otherwise happen to both parties. Tiffin ended by expressing the hope that the Great Spirit would "incline your hearts and the hearts of your people to peace." A month later, Tecumseh assured the governor that he and his people had no intention of causing "any disturbance with the white people."[25]

A Prophecy Come True

The Prophet, meanwhile, had been gathering both followers and enemies. Even some Shawnee chiefs were calling him—and Tecumseh—dangerous. The Prophet did not like the idea of any Indian—Shawnee or otherwise—opposing him and set out to stop them. He told his followers that anyone who opposed him was selfish and was standing in the way of the common good of all Indian nations. Such people, he declared, were possessed by evil spirits and had to die. So the Prophet accused any of his people who opposed him of one kind of witchcraft or another and had them killed. When Tecumseh found out, he was horrified and made it clear that there should be no more such killings.

All this time, William Henry Harrison, the governor of Indiana, was keeping an

A Council at Springfield

In his book, Colonel W. S. Hatch describes the role Tecumseh played at an 1806 council held at Springfield. In this excerpt, quoted in The Indian Tribes Historically Considered, *Hatch summarizes the Shawnee leader's speech.*

"All was apparently going on satisfactorily, when Tecumtha arose and commenced his address; he continued his oration for three hours; commencing with the first aggressions of the white men, and bringing down his traditional history from the first settlement at Plymouth and Jamestown to his own time. The effect of his bitter, burning words of eloquence was so great on his companions, that the whole three hundred could hardly refrain from springing from their seats. Their eyes flashed, and even the most aged, many of whom were smoking, evinced the greatest excitement. The orator appeared in all the power of a fiery and impassioned speaker and actor.

At the conclusion of his address, Tecumtha stood for a moment, turned his back upon the agent's stand, and walking to the circle opposite, took his seat among the young braves, glancing with pride upon the agents."

eye on the Prophet. Like Tecumseh, he was horrified by news of the witch hunts. He thought the power and leadership belonged not to Tecumseh but to Tenskwatawa and was determined to block him. In April 1806 Harrison sent a message to the Delawares begging them to renounce their support for the Prophet. In the letter warning them about Tenskwatawa, he asked,

> Who is this pretended prophet, who dares to speak in the name of the Great Creator? Examine him. Is he more wise or virtuous than you are yourselves, that he should be selected to convey to you the orders of your God? . . . Demand of him some proofs at least, of his being the messenger of the Deity. If God has really employed him, he has doubtless authorized him to perform miracles, that he may be known and received as a prophet. . . . If he is really a prophet, ask of him to cause the sun to stand still—the moon to alter its course—the rivers to cease to flow—or the dead to rise from their graves. If he does these things, you may then believe he has been sent from God.[26]

The Prophet answered the challenge. Somehow Tecumseh had learned that on June 16, 1806, there would be an eclipse of the sun. He passed this information on to his brother, who announced that at noon on June 16 he, Tenskwatawa, would send Mukutaaweethee Keesohtoa, "the dreaded Black Sun." The Prophet invited everyone to come watch as he caused the sun to darken, and people flocked to the gathering place. At 11:32 A.M., the Prophet pointed to the sun. As he did so, the moon began to move slowly across its face.

In addition to his loyal followers, the Prophet also acquired many powerful enemies. In 1806, Governor Harrison pleaded with the Delaware to denounce Tenskwatawa as a fraud.

Greenville got so dark that fowl roosted for the night and nocturnal animals came scurrying from their hiding places. For seven minutes, it was pitch dark. Then the Prophet begged the Master of Life to take his hand away from the face of the sun and make it bright again. Soon the eclipse was over, and the sun shone as brightly as it had earlier.

The eclipse had fulfilled the Prophet's prophecy that a blanket of darkness would cover the land. The story of the "miracle" was passed from person to person, and the fame of the Prophet spread across the land. Word of him reached the ears of the Ottawa and

Ojibwa and from there traveled south to the Creek and Cherokee and west to the Ponca, Mandan, Blackfoot, and Sioux. As the news of Tenskwatawa's power spread, the number of his followers grew. Most found their way to Greenville. But now the respect the Prophet commanded was tinged with fear.

Tecumseh encouraged his brother's followers. They could make a united Indian nation a reality. The Prophet's followers had faith in him and in each other. Once again they took great pride in who they were—North American Indians. This faith and pride that brought the different nations together at Greenville would make them into one distinct people, united and strong. Imagine—all Indian nations across the land, from Florida to Canada, joined together into a mighty alliance, one strong nation that refused to give up its land or sign any more treaties! Never before had the Indian nations in North America been united as one. In 1675 the Wampanoag chief Metacom, whom the whites called King Philip, had forged the first great Indian alliance. Later, in 1763, the Ottawa chief Pontiac had led many Indian nations in an uprising against the British. Pontiac had drawn supporters from nations as far east as the Seneca in western New York and as far west as the Sioux. But even he had not united them all.

Above all, Tecumseh believed that his people would survive only if they were united. His passion for his cause was endless. He knew that without unity, the culture of his people would one day cease to exist. Years later the Prophet was to say that his brother's plans were "to embody all the Indian tribes in a grand confederacy, from the province of Mexico, to the Great Lakes, to unite their forces in an army that would be able to meet and drive back the white people, who were continually advancing on the Indian tribes, and forcing them from their lands towards the Rocky Mountains."[27]

A Meeting at Adena

Meanwhile, things were not going well between the Americans and the British. Indiana governor Harrison worried that once again the two sides would be at war. He was convinced that the British were storing ammunition in Greenville. He shared his fears with the governor of Ohio, who sent representatives to ask why followers of the Prophet were in the village. The governor invited Tecumseh and some of the other Indian leaders to meet with him and other U.S. officials in a general council in Chillicothe in 1807. The council was held at Adena, the new home of Ohio senator Thomas Worthington.

Tecumseh spoke for almost three hours, reviewing one by one all the Ohio land treaties, including the one signed at Greenville. None of the treaties were valid, he argued. The whites had no legal claim to the lands north and west of the Ohio. The people who had made the treaties did not own the land. What right did they have, he asked, to give away what they did not own? Tecumseh made it clear that he would do whatever was necessary to keep whites from moving onto Indian land. But he said it in such a way that Governor Tiffin and his aides thought that the Shawnee's intentions were peaceful. They were sure he did not intend to make war.

The Prophet performs an incantation before Governor Harrison. Despite the governor's attempts to discredit Tenskwatawa, Tecumseh and the Prophet continued to attract supporters.

Harrison and the Bad Birds

Tecumseh's speech at Adena may have made the others feel safe. But William Henry Harrison still believed that the British were telling the Prophet what to do. Not long after the meeting in Chillicothe, he sent a message to the Shawnee chiefs reminding them of the Greenville treaty and warning them against the Prophet. The Indiana governor was blunt: "You have," Harrison told the chiefs, "called in a number of men from the most distant tribes to listen to a fool, who speaks not the words of the Great Spirit but those of the devil and of the British agents."[28]

The Prophet was angry when he heard how Harrison had tried to influence the chiefs. He concealed that anger when he responded to Harrison, however, addressing the governor with pretended respect:

Father, I am sorry that you listen to the advice of bad birds. You have impeached me with [accused me of] having correspondence with the British, and with calling and sending for the Indians from the most distant parts of the country 'to listen to a fool that speaks not the words of the Great

Spirit, but the words of the devil.' Father, these impeachments I deny, and say they are not true. I never had a word with the British, and I never sent for the Indians. They came here themselves to listen and hear the words of the Great Spirit. Father, I wish you would not listen any more to the voice of bad birds; . . . it is the least of our idea to make disturbances, and we will rather try to stop such proceedings than encourage them.[29]

An Incident at Adena

During the 1807 visit to Adena, an incident occurred that showed clearly the power and dignity of Tecumseh in what could have been an unfortunate event. Mrs. Anna Shannon McAllister, who described the incident, is quoted in Blue Jacket *by John Bennett.*

"The Senator [Thomas Worthington] invited the celebrated Tecumseh and other warriors, among them Blue Jacket, to spend a few nights with him at Adena. Consternation reigned in the household when this savage retinue appeared; but all were charged to ignore any eccentricity [strangeness] of manners, and to trust to the good discipline which Tecumseh was known to have over his followers.

The Indians, at least Tecumseh, is said to have joined easily in the amenities [polite customs] of home life at Adena. He made but one exception; he refused to sleep indoors, but camped out at night on the ground.

Though she strove to make them welcome, my lady Eleanor [Mrs. Worthington] took her place at the table each midday with no little trepidation [concern]. Her guests seated themselves with perfect propriety [good manners], and serenity reigned until one day there was a sudden commotion and two or three of the young braves leaped angrily to their feet. Tecumseh was in close conversation with his host, but observing Mrs. Worthington's look of alarm, arose with superb dignity and with a glance and a stamp of his foot restored instant order. Quite by accident the hostess had failed to serve coffee to one of the young bucks, no small insult in his eyes. This disturbing incident was the only one to mar the harmony of the visit, and the unusual guests departed highly pleased with their entertainment [the hospitality they had received]."

A Message and a Move

By this time Tecumseh was almost forty years old. He was still muscular and powerful, and his hazel eyes were still sharp. But his face was harder looking and his temper flared more quickly. One spring day in 1807 Anthony Shane, whose mother was Shawnee, came to see him. Tecumseh and Shane had grown up together in Chillicothe. Shane had brought a message from William Wells, the government agent in Fort Wayne, ordering Tecumseh and the Prophet to come to Fort Wayne to receive a message from President Thomas Jefferson. Wells was no stranger to Tecumseh. Captured and adopted by the Miamis when in his teens, Wells had not only lived with the Miami for more than eight years, he had fought with them and with the Shawnees against the whites. But Wells had angered Tecumseh by deserting his Indian brothers to work for the U.S. government. Tecumseh refused to go to Fort Wayne, saying that in six days he would call a council and Wells could come to the village then and deliver the message in person.

Wells, like Harrison, was sure that the Prophet was planning to make war on the white settlements. Afraid to go to the council himself, he sent Shane instead. Shane was supposed to tell Tecumseh and the Prophet that since the Shawnee living at Greenville had no right to be there, on land belonging to the government of the United States, they had to move at once. Neither Wells nor Shane knew that Tecumseh already had plans to leave the area. Food supplies were low, there were too many white settlements nearby, and Governor Harrison was sending his spies into Greenville. (How else could he know about every move the Shawnee made?) But Wells had made Tecumseh so angry that he decided to put off the relocation. "These lands," he argued, "are ours! No one has the right to remove us because we were the first owners. The Great Spirit above has appointed this place for us, on which to light our fires, and here we will remain. As to boundaries, the Great Spirit above knows no boundaries, nor will his red children acknowledge any."[30]

Not until the spring of 1808 did the people of Tecumseh's village at Greenville finally begin their move. They built canoes to carry them down the Mississinewa to the Wabash. There, on the high ground of the northern bank of the river, they built a new settlement. The land lay a couple of miles downstream from the mouth of the Tippecanoe River, near what is today Lafayette, Indiana. The Indian nations called the land Kehtipaquononk—"the great clearing." A large Shawnee village that had once sat there had been destroyed by U.S. officials in 1791. The new village was called Tippecanoe by some and Prophetstown by others. There was wild game in the forest, and fish were plentiful in the rivers. Here Tecumseh, Tenskwatawa, and their followers built an entirely new village, complete with strong cabins, *wigewas*, a large lodge for visitors, a medicine lodge for the Prophet, and a huge council house of logs and bark.

Chapter

6 Endless Conflict

Now that Prophetstown was established, Tecumseh knew that his and his brother's followers would have a safe retreat, away from the prying eyes and ears of William Henry Harrison's spies. Now Tecumseh felt he could travel the country to promote Indian unity. But first he had to go to Canada to a council called by the British at Fort Malden, their outpost at Amherstburg, about fifteen miles from Detroit. The British knew that if war broke out again with the Americans, they would need the Indian nations on their side. Tecumseh told the British general in charge of the fort that he and his followers did not want to get caught up in any quarrels between whites. But, he went on to say, if the Americans kept intruding on his people's lands, they would strike. And if, at that time, the British king wanted to send more troops, Tecumseh and his followers would support the effort.

Spreading the Word

The talks at Amherstburg over, Tecumseh could go on his journey and convince people to band together as one to protect and defend what was rightfully theirs.

First Tecumseh went among the Wyandot, the Sac and Fox, the Seneca, and the Winnebago, urging them all to join with him. In the spring of 1808 he crossed the central plains, speaking passionately at each stop, working to get each group he visited excited about forming a union. Again and again he spoke to Indian nations along the Illinois River and in Wis-

Over a period of four years, Tecumseh traveled among the many North American Indian nations, urging them to unite against the whites. Tecumseh's provocative words caused many young warriors to answer his call to arms.

consin. That autumn he made the first of many journeys to speak to the Indian nations of the old Northwest Territory and the south. He went to Florida to talk to the Seminoles, to Missouri to recruit the Osage, to New York to spread the word to the Iroquois.

For four years or so, Tecumseh traveled from one group of Indians to another. He traveled on foot, by canoe, on horseback. He covered thousands of miles. Not everyone accepted his ideas. Older chiefs had listened to what he had to say, but many of them could not go along with his call to arms. It was a different story, though, with the young warriors. Most of them had been excited by his powerful words and his plans for an Indian nation. Tecumseh did not always succeed, but he always made those who heard him think about things they had not stopped to think about before.

A Treaty at Fort Wayne

At the same time Tecumseh was trying to unite his people, his adversary William Henry Harrison was working to make Indiana a state. As long as most of the land belonged to the Indians and was not legally open to settlement by whites, however, he would fall short of the sixty thousand free white citizens needed to apply for statehood. Harrison's goal was to convince the Indian nations to turn over about three million acres of land.

Thomas Jefferson wanted land for Americans. He envisioned a nation of industrious farmers, helping the United States grow and prosper. For this to happen, white settlers had to be able to move

President Thomas Jefferson's dreams of westward expansion conflicted with the desires of the Indians to remain on their ancestral homelands.

farther westward. The land, thought Jefferson, should belong to those who were able and wanted to develop it. With the following questions, he made clear how he felt about the situation:

What is the right of a huntsman to the thousand miles over which he has accidentally ranged in search of prey? Is one of the fairest portions of the globe to remain in a state of nature, the haunt of a few wretched savages, when it seems destined by the Creator to give support to a large population, and to be the seat of civilization, of science and true religion?[31]

Jefferson's belief that Indians were savages who were not the equal of whites was not unique to him. In his times, most whites thought they were superior to other races and ethnic groups. Jefferson, sincerely believing that white settlers would put the land to better use than the Indians, had a plan to legally free it up for whites while giving Native Americans a chance to share in his vision of the United States. He would give the Indians an opportunity to become farmers. If they grew disgusted with farming or failed at it, they would be willing to sign the land over to the whites. Jefferson angered the chiefs of the Indian nations, telling them that "nothing is so easy to learn as to cultivate the earth—all your women understand it."[32]

William Henry Harrison set out to get the land the president wanted. First, Harrison offered bribes—rolls of red cloth, food, and other presents—to chiefs he thought would agree to a new treaty. Then he invited them and representatives of certain other Indian nations to a great council to be held at Fort Wayne. Among those invited were the Miamis, loyal friends of the United States who had lived along the Wabash for years; the Delawares, newcomers to the Indiana Territory; and the Potawatomis, who lived far north of the lands Harrison wanted and were very poor. Harrison knew the Shawnee—and probably the Kickapoo—would argue against the treaty, so he did not invite them.

More than a thousand Indians came to the council at Fort Wayne. On September 30, 1809, the chiefs signed a treaty that gave Harrison what is today most of south-central Indiana—three million acres. In return, those who signed received about $10,000. The chiefs could not read the treaty, so U.S. officials drew them a map of the land in question. Much of it was not owned or even hunted on by the chiefs who had signed it away. Although the Prophet had spies who kept him informed, he did nothing to oppose the treaty. Instead, he sat silent while the Shawnee lost some of their best hunting grounds. Tecumseh was traveling along the Mississippi River when the council was called and the treaty signed. As soon as he got back to Prophetstown, he called an emergency council to tell the people about the treaty.

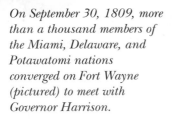

On September 30, 1809, more than a thousand members of the Miami, Delaware, and Potawatomi nations converged on Fort Wayne (pictured) to meet with Governor Harrison.

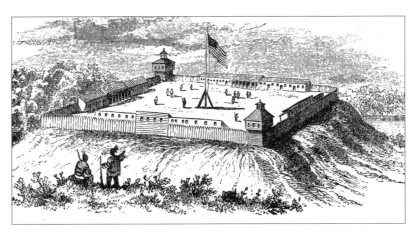

While some Indians chose to live in cabins like whites, many more clung to their traditional ways and continued to live in wigwams.

The Aftermath

By the spring of 1810, more than a thousand warriors—Shawnee, Sac and Fox, Miami, Kickapoo, Delaware, Potawatomi, Ottawa, Chippewa—had gathered at Prophetstown. Hundreds of bark wigwams dotted the slope that ran upward from the river. In May Tecumseh visited Wapakoneta, a Shawnee village in Ohio. The village chief Catahecassa—"Black Hoof"—had cast his lot with the Americans long before and was no friend to Tecumseh. He believed his people should adopt the ways of the whites. So instead of living in wigwams, the people of Wapakoneta lived in cabins; instead of hunting, they tilled the soil and raised pigs and cattle. Black Hoof refused to meet with Tecumseh. But the young men of the village came to hear what he had to say. With them was the former Sinnantha, Stephen Ruddell. Now a Christian minister and a missionary, Ruddell was teaching the villagers to live as whites. Tecumseh began to speak, but Ruddell interrupted him to read aloud a letter from William Henry Harrison. Tecumseh grabbed the paper from the hand of his one-time playmate and threw it into the fire. By the end of the speech, many of the young warriors had promised to join Tecumseh at Prophetstown in the fall.

Standoff at Vincennes

Governor Harrison grew more concerned by the day. He knew that Tecumseh's reputation had been growing among the Indian nations, bringing him and the Prophet more followers. Many Indians had grown bolder, and horse theft and raids against the settlers kept increasing. Harrison also knew that Tecumseh believed that the chiefs who had signed the treaty at Fort Wayne had no right to do so.

Harrison's biggest fear was that Tecumseh would lead the Indians to war against the Americans.

Harrison wanted to show Tecumseh the strength of the Americans and the foolishness of his way of thinking. In a letter he wrote to the Shawnee brothers, Harrison said:

> What reason have you to complain of the Seventeen Fires? Have they ever violated the treaties made with the red men? You say they have purchased land from those who had no right to sell them. Show that this is true and the land will be instantly restored. Show us the rightful owners.[33]

Still believing that the Prophet, not Tecumseh, was the power among the Indians, Governor Harrison invited the Prophet and three chiefs to go to Washington to meet with the president. Later the messenger wrote that Tecumseh was "really the efficient man—the Moses of the family . . . described by all as a bold, active, sensible man, daring in the extreme and capable of any undertaking."[34]

The Prophet and Tecumseh accepted the governor's invitation. On August 11, 1810, accompanied by three hundred warriors, they set off down the Wabash in eighty canoes to meet with Harrison. The meeting was to be at Vincennes, once a French village, now the capital of Indiana Territory. The faces of the braves, covered with red war paint, were set and hard, and in the canoes were tomahawks and war clubs. According to a captain from Fort Knox who stopped them a few miles from Vincennes, Tecumseh was "one of the finest looking men I ever saw—about six feet high, straight, with large, fine features, and altogether a daring boldlooking fellow."[35]

The Prophet had been to Vincennes twice before, once in 1808 and once in 1809. The last time, Harrison had asked him about a failed plot by the British and some Indian allies. After that meeting, Harrison wrote to the U.S. secretary of war that his "suspicions of [the Prophet's] guilt have been rather strengthened than diminished at every interview I have had with him since his arrival."[36]

Harrison had planned to hold the meeting on a canopied porch at the side of his headquarters. But Tecumseh had refused to meet there. "Houses," he said, "are made for white men to hold their councils in; Indians hold theirs in the open air." Harrison pointed to one of the chairs that had been set up. "Your father," he said quietly, "requests you to take a chair." Tecumseh looked at the chair, walked away, and sat down under the shade of some trees in a grove not far from the house. "My father?" he said sharply. "The Sun is my father, and the earth is my mother, and in her bosom I will repose."[37]

They met in the tree-shaded grove—Harrison in his uniform trimmed in gold braid, Harrison's people, the Prophet, thirty warriors, and Tecumseh in his buckskin leggings and shirt, a red blanket draped around his shoulders, two eagle feathers in his hair. Speaking in his native tongue, Tecumseh named each treaty and told how unfair it had been. He spoke of how his people had been killed and how their land had been taken from them. He spoke too of the spoiled food they had been given and of the many who had died from diseases brought by the whites.

> It is true that I am a Shawnee. My forefathers were warriors. Their son is a

Tecumseh and his entourage meet with Governor Harrison in the shady grove at Vincennes.

warrior. From them I only take my existence; from my tribe I take nothing. . . . The being within . . . tells me, that once, nor until lately, there was no white man on this continent, that it then all belonged to red men . . . placed on it by the Great Spirit that made them, to keep it and to fill it with the same race. Once a happy race. Since made miserable by the white race who are never contented but always encroaching.

The way, and the only way, to check and stop this evil is for all the red men to unite in claiming a common and equal right in the land, as it was at first, and should be yet. It was never divided, but belongs to all, for the use of each. That no part has a right to sell, even to each other, much less to strangers, those who want all, and will not do with less. The white people have no right to take the land from the Indians, because they had it first; it is theirs. They may sell, but all must join. Any sale not made by all is not valid. The late sale is bad. It was made by a part only. . . . It requires all to make a bargain for all. All red men have equal rights to the unoccupied land. The right of occupancy is as good in one place as in another. There cannot be two occupations in the same place. The first excludes all others. It is not so in hunting or travelling; for there the same ground will serve many . . . but the camp is stationary, and that is occupancy. It belongs to the first who sits down on his blanket or skins,

Declaration at Vincennes

In 1872, in his book about the War of 1812, Colonel W. S. Hatch of the Cincinnati Light Infantry wrote about his impressions of Tecumseh at the 1810 meeting at Vincennes.

"[Tecumseh] asserted his policy openly and fully, that he was forming a grand confederacy of all the nations and tribes of Indians upon the continent, for the purpose of putting a stop to the encroachments of the white people; and in his argument in defense of his course, said that 'the policy which the United States pursued of purchasing in unceasing detail their lands from the separate Indian tribes, he viewed as a mighty water ready to overflow his people, and that the confederacy which he was forming among the tribes to prevent any individual tribe from selling without the consent of the others, was the dam he was erecting to resist this mighty water.'"

which he has thrown upon the ground, and till he leaves it no other has a right.[38]

When Tecumseh finished speaking, Harrison replied that when the white people came, the Shawnee lived in Georgia, while the land around the Wabash River was occupied by the Miamis. The Americans, he said, had bought the lands from the Miamis, "the true and original owners of it." He argued that it was "ridiculous" to say that all the Indians were one nation. "If such had been the intention of the Great Spirit, he would not have put six different tongues into their heads, but would have taught them all to speak one language."[39]

Tecumseh listened while Harrison insisted that the Shawnee "had no right to come from a distant country to control the Miamis in the disposal of their own property."[40] Then Harrison, who had ad-

mitted to the secretary of war that all whites did not treat the Indians justly, said that the United States had always dealt fairly with the Indians. At this point, Tecumseh lost patience. His people, he warned, would die before they gave up their land and way of life. In their minds, the treaties were worthless pieces of paper. When he called Harrison a liar, the governor drew his sword and told Tecumseh to get out.

The next morning Tecumseh apologized and invited Harrison to sit next to him on a bench. Tecumseh moved closer to Harrison. Harrison moved away a little. Tecumseh kept moving closer and Harrison away until Harrison cried, "See, Tecumseh, you are crowding me off!" "Ah," said Tecumseh, "that exactly explains our grief—you whites are crowding us Indians a little by little, and we don't know where we shall in the end be crowded to."[41]

The next day Harrison told Tecumseh that any decision in the matter would have to come from the president, who probably would not give back the lands. To this Tecumseh replied sharply, "As the great chief over the mountains is to decide the matter, I hope the Great Spirit will put sense enough in his head to order you to give up those lands. It is true, he is so far off, he will not be injured by the war. He may sit in his fine house and drink his wine while you and I have to fight it out."[42]

Angrily Harrison announced that the meeting was at an end. Knowing that no more would be accomplished, Tecumseh left. Harrison could not forget, though, that Tecumseh had said he was going to visit the Indian nations in the south and that the treaty was evil, false, and

without meaning. . . . It was signed by a few, poor, weak, foolish, worn-out chiefs who have no rights any more among the Indians. All is now in the hands of the warriors. . . . The land which the false treaty gave away has not been returned to its true owners, the Indians, we shall kill those chiefs. It will be your hand which is red with their blood.[43]

At home, Harrison sent a letter to the secretary of war, warning him that "there can be no doubt that [Tecumseh's] object is to excite the southern Indians to war." Describing Tecumseh's power, he wrote:

The implicit obedience and respect which the followers of Tecumseh pay him is really astonishing, and more than any other circumstance bespeaks him as one of those uncommon geniuses which spring up occasionally to produce revolutions and overturn the established order of things. . . . If it were not for the vicinity of the United States [Tecumseh] would, perhaps, be the founder of an empire that would rival in glory Mexico or Peru. No difficulties deter him. For four years he

During their meeting at Vincennes, Tecumseh called Governor Harrison a liar. The accusation caused Harrison to draw his sword and demand that Tecumseh leave.

had been in constant motion. You see him today on the Wabash, and in a short time hear of him on the shores of Lake Erie or on the banks of the Mississippi; and wherever he goes he makes an impression favorable to his purposes.[44]

A Time of Tension

After Vincennes, Harrison was even more sure that he had to do something about Prophetstown. Each day more people from different Indian nations gathered

Tecumseh's Truth at Vincennes

Tecumseh had much to say at Vincennes when he met with Governor Harrison. This brief excerpt from the speech he made about the recent treaty is quoted in The Heroes of Defeat.

"Brother, this land that was sold and the goods that were given for it was done by only a few. You have said that if we could show that, the land was sold by people who had no right to sell, you would restore it. It was. These tribes set up a claim, but the tribes with me will not agree to their claim. If the lands are not restored to us, you will see when we return home how it will be settled. We shall have a grand council at which all the tribes will be present, when we will show to those disposing of the lands that they had no right to the claim they set up. We will see what will be done to those chiefs that did sell the land to you. I am not alone in this determination. It is the determination of all the warriors and chiefs who listen to me. I am authorized by all the tribes to tell you this. I am the head of them all. I am a warrior and all the warriors will call for all those chiefs who parted with that land and, if you do not restore it, you will have a hand in killing them. We do not come here to get presents from you. By taking goods from you, you will say that with them you purchased another piece of land from us. It has been the object of both myself and my brethren to prevent lands from being sold. If you cross the boundaries of our present settlements, it will cause great trouble among us. How can we have confidence in the white people? When Jesus Christ was on earth, you killed him. You nailed him on a cross. You thought he was dead, but you were mistaken."

After realizing that a peaceful resolution was no longer possible, Tecumseh traveled to Fort Malden (pictured) to forge a partnership with the British.

there. He planned on spending the winter thinking about what he would do.

Almost a year passed. Even though tensions kept mounting, no decisions were reached. In June 1811 Tecumseh traveled briefly to western Michigan to rally more Potawatomi and Ottawa to his cause. He sent messengers across the Mississippi to meet with the Iowa and to Ontario, Canada, to meet with the Mohawk.

In July two Potawatomi killed some white settlers in Illinois. Harrison said that the murderers were followers of the Prophet and ordered that they be turned over at once. Tecumseh, he said, must come to Vincennes to explain the incident and place the killers in Harrison's custody. Tecumseh took several hundred warriors with him to Vincennes, where they encountered eight hundred militiamen and soldiers on patrol. The Shawnee chief refused to turn over the Potawatomi. Why,

Tecumseh asked, were whites who murdered his people allowed to go free, and Indians who killed whites punished? He told Harrison that he wanted whites and Indians to live together side by side in peace and harmony. It was the last time Tecumseh ever talked of peace with the Long Knives.

Deciding that the time had come to speak to the British, Tecumseh headed north to Fort Malden. Relations between Britain and the United States were bad, and Tecumseh knew that soon he would have to side with one or the other. He was sure that the destiny of his people depended on the Americans' losing. At Fort Malden, Tecumseh told the British about the confederation he was building, pointing out, as well, that his people would need arms and supplies if and when war broke out between England and the United States. Showing the British a wampum belt given to the chiefs who in past years had helped the British defeat the French, Tecumseh stated exactly where he stood and what he expected:

> You, Father, have nourished us, and raised us up from Childhood. We are now Men and think ourselves capable of defending our Country. I intend proceeding towards the Mid Day sun and expect before next Autumn and before I visit you again, that the business will be done. I request Father that you will be charitable to our King, Women and Children. The Young Men can more easily provide for themselves than they.[45]

But since the British were not yet ready to go to war, Tecumseh had to be content with a pack train of supplies that arrived in the fall.

South Again

In early August 1811, Tecumseh set off with several dozen warriors on a six-month-long journey of a thousand miles. Before he left Prophetstown, he gave his brother strict orders. Under no circumstances, Tecumseh warned, should Tenskwatawa or his followers do anything to anger Harrison—Prophetstown had had enough troubles that year, including drought, ruined crops, and little game. No matter what happened, he emphasized, no one from Prophetstown was to attack the Americans. The Prophet agreed and promised to be careful to avoid any act likely to excite the whites.

That settled, Tecumseh was ready to begin the journey south. He had ordered the braves to dress in buckskin and carry tomahawks and scalping knives to show that they were Indian warriors who depended on Indian weapons and lived according to Indian ways. Except for scalp-locks that hung to their shoulders in three long braids, their heads were shaved. Around their foreheads they wore wide bright red flannel bands with silver dots and hawk feathers sticking up. They had painted red circles on their foreheads and red slashes below their eyes and across their cheekbones. Silver collars and bands adorned their throats and wrists. Tecumseh wore two crane feathers, a white one to show that he came in peace and a red one to show that he was ready for war.

Tecumseh and the others headed down the Wabash to the Ohio and Mississippi Rivers, through Tennessee to Mississippi, Alabama, Georgia, and Florida. Most of the Indian nations of the south were rich and comfortable, so they were not very eager for war—except for the Seminoles of Florida. Tecumseh told the Seminoles, as well as some others, that a ship would appear off the Florida coast. The ship, he said, would be commanded by the British and would be filled with guns, ammunition, and supplies. After the braves got the supplies, they were to head north to meet Tecumseh. To make sure the chiefs would know exactly when to act, Tecumseh gave each chief a bundle of red-painted sticks. "Each time the moon is full," he told them, "burn one stick. When the last stick is burned, the Great Spirit will give you a sign. Then gather your warriors and march north to meet me."[46]

From Florida Tecumseh and the others headed back north—to the Carolinas, to the Ozark Mountains of Arkansas and

Missouri, to Iowa, and finally home. He had visited with many different groups and had spoken with passion and strength to each.

"Where today are the Pequot?," he had asked. "Where are the Narragansett, the Mohican, the Pokanoket, and many other once powerful tribes of our people? They have vanished," he cried, "before the avarice [greed] and oppression of the White Man, as snow before a summer sun." Of each he asked, "Will we let ourselves be destroyed in our turn without a struggle, give up our homes, our country bequeathed to us by the Great Spirit, the graves of our dead and everything that is dear and sacred to us?" Now he drove home his point—"I know you will cry with me, 'Never! Never!'"[47]

Tecumseh told the Choctaw and Chickasaw to look over the once beautiful country and tell him what they saw. You will see, he cried, "nothing but the ruins of the paleface destroyers!" . . . "So it will be with you . . . !" he warned. "Soon your

---

Misunderstanding at Vincennes

In his memoirs, quoted in History of the Indian Tribes of North America, *William Henry Harrison spoke of what happened at Vincennes the morning after his quarrel with Tecumseh.*

"Tecumthé presented himself with the same undaunted bearing which always marked him as a superior man; but he was now dignified and collected, and showed no disposition to resume his former insolent deportment [rude behavior]. He disclaimed having entertained any intention of attacking the governor, but said he had been advised by two white men to do as he had done. Two white men—British emissaries undoubtedly—had visited him at his place of residence, and told him that half the white people were opposed to the governor, and willing to relinquish the land, and urged him to advise the tribes not to receive pay for it, alleging that the governor would soon be recalled, and a good man put in his place, who would give up the land to the Indians. He replied, that he was determined to adhere to the *old boundary.* Then arose a Wyandot, a Kickapoo, a Potawatomi, an Ottawa, and a Winnebago chief, each declaring his determination to stand by Tecumthé. The governor then said, that the words of Tecumthé should be reported to the President, who would take measures to enforce the treaty; and the council ended."

Tecumseh's passionate speeches gained him the respect of Native Americans and whites alike.

mighty forests will be cut down to fence in the land which the white intruders dare to call their own!"[48]

Tecumseh reminded the Creeks that they had been a mighty people and told them that now their tomahawks had no edge and their bows and arrows were buried with their fathers. He urged them to "brush from your eyes the sleep of slavery! Once more strike for vengeance—once more for your country!"[49] It was at this time that Tecumseh predicted the great New Madrid earthquake of 1811. In his parting words at the Creek village of Tuckhabatchee, Tecumseh warned that when he reached Detroit he would stamp his foot on the ground and shake down all the houses in the village. He had been insulted by the chief's refusal to approve the confederation after having agreed to do so.

A white who had fought against the Indian nations, hearing Tecumseh speak in Mississippi, wrote that

> his eyes burned with supernatural luster, and his whole frame trembled with emotion. His voice resounded over the multitude—now sinking in low and musical whispers, now rising to the highest key, hurling out his words like a succession of thunderbolts. I have heard many great orators, . . . but I never saw one with the vocal powers of Tecumseh.[50]

Conflict at Tippecanoe

William Henry Harrison had been making plans ever since the meeting at Vincennes. He had sent many letters to James Madison, the new president, warning him that the Indians on the Wabash were a threat. When Tecumseh's prophecy had come true, with an earthquake striking the Mississippi Valley and the Mississippi River turning and flowing north for a while, many Indians were convinced of Tecumseh's powers. Hundreds had headed for Detroit and the confederation. Raids on whites had grown in number and in ferocity.

President Madison knew what was going on with the Indians and on the frontier. But he was more worried about American-British relations. He warned Harrison not to cause trouble and not to act unless the Prophet's people attacked the Americans. Harrison, meanwhile, plagued by demands from whites on the border of the Wabash to remove the Prophet and his followers, ignored the president's advice. The minute he found out that Tecumseh had headed south, he made his move. Harrison's plan was to march his army to Prophetstown and get rid of the Prophet and Tecumseh's dream. About a thousand infantry soldiers, the brass buttons on their blue uniforms shining, and red, white, and blue feathers adding color to their stovetop hats, marched from Vincennes. On October 6, 1811, Harrison had a stockade built on the Wabash about sixty-five miles from Vincennes. About a month later, he rode out with nine hundred men and headed for Prophetstown.

There were about 450 warriors in Prophetstown when Tenskwatawa's scouts came to tell him that hundreds of Long Knives had crossed the Wabash River and were marching out of the woods about a mile west of town. At once the Prophet sent warriors with a white flag to find Harrison and give him the following message: The Prophet wanted a truce and would meet with Harrison the next day to try to reach a peaceful settlement. Against the advice of his officers, Harrison agreed. Then the Americans set up camp on a piece of high ground that rose out of a marshy prairie. While they were making camp, militant Winnebago warriors convinced the Prophet to order an attack. Ignoring his promise to Tecumseh, the Prophet gathered together the young braves among his followers and told them that if they attacked the Long Knives he would use his magic to protect them. He said that there were not a great many soldiers in the enemy camp, and some were already dead. He said that he would make the whites as harmless as sand and cause their bullets to turn to water. He gave his word that no Indian would be killed and that Harrison's army would be wiped out.

Harrison had laid out his camp in the shape of a rectangle, with the horses and wagons in the center and strong outposts around the edge. With orders to kill Harrison and his senior officers, black-painted warriors crawled on their stomachs through the American lines. It was about four o'clock in the morning, the seventh of November, bitterly cold and rainy. But a

Ignoring the president's orders, William Henry Harrison marched his troops toward Prophetstown in November 1811.

sentry saw the attackers and got off a shot before he was killed. The warriors who had already made it into the camp were fighting the Long Knives hand to hand. Meanwhile, the other warriors attacked, not once but three times, each time putting themselves within point-blank range of enemy guns. While Harrison urged his men on, the Prophet stayed safely on a hill, well away from American bullets and bayonets. When the action began, he "entered upon the performance of certain mystic rites, at the same time singing a war-song. In the course of the engagement, he was informed that his men were falling: he told them to fight on—it would soon be as he had predicted; and then, in louder and wilder strains, his inspiring battle-song was heard commingling with the sharp crack of the rifle and the shrill war-whoop of his brave but deluded followers."[51]

The fighting went on for about two hours. When it was over, victory belonged to the U.S. troops. The last bayonet charge had sent the remaining warriors running into the nearby swampland. Almost none of the whites seemed to care that Harrison had deliberately marched an army onto Indian land to provoke a fight.

Tecumseh returned to Prophetstown a few days after the battle. What had been a lively village was now a pile of remains and ashes. Sticking out of the snow was what was left of the council house. Harrison had torched the deserted village, the

Warriors from Prophetstown fall to the Long Knives' bullets during the fierce Battle of Tippecanoe. After defeating the Indians, Harrison and his troops torched Prophetstown, reducing the once bustling village to ashes.

Jefferson Speaks Out

President Thomas Jefferson thought he knew exactly how to get Indian lands legally. In a letter to William Henry Harrison, taken from A Sorrow in Our Heart, *he explained his plan.*

"When they [the Indians] withdraw themselves to the culture of a small piece of earth, they will perceive how useless to them are extensive forests and will be willing to pare them off in exchange for necessaries for their farms and families. To promote this, we shall push our trading houses, and be glad to see the good and influential individuals among them in debt, because we observe that when these debts get beyond what the individual can pay, they become willing to lop them off by a cession of lands. But should any tribe refuse the proffered hand and take up the hatchet, it will be driven across the Mississippi and the whole of its lands confiscated."

fields, and the thousands of bushels of corn the villagers had harvested and hidden in the woods. The Battle of Tippecanoe had been a disaster for Tecumseh's cause and a triumph for Harrison. Later, when he had become president of the United States, Harrison bragged to William Eustice, his secretary of war, that "the Indians had never sustained so severe a defeat since their acquaintance with the white people."[52] A Kentucky lawyer who knew Harrison remarked acidly that Harrison's "vanity more than fermented, it blubbered over."[53]

7 A New Alliance

The Battle of Tippecanoe changed many things for the Prophet, for Tecumseh, and for their followers. But what was to come after—a war between the Americans and the British—would have a far greater and longer-lasting effect.

After Tippecanoe

Tecumseh blamed the Prophet for the Battle of Tippecanoe. If only he had kept his word not to provoke Harrison while Tecumseh was away, the battle would not have occurred, Prophetstown would still be standing, and the people would not have lost faith in their leaders. Furious, Tecumseh banished his brother to the wilderness. Tenskwatawa's influence was gone, and so was his career as a prophet. He headed west and, in time, moved to Kansas, where he died in 1837.

The Battle of Tippecanoe was a big setback for Tecumseh. He had worked very hard to unite his people and had not wanted to fight the whites until he was sure the confederation was strong enough to succeed. The fight had come too soon, and now the Indians who had been at Prophetstown were spread far and wide. Some had turned away from Tecumseh

entirely. Prophetstown—the gathering place, the physical center—was gone too.

In another way, though, Tippecanoe had made some things clearer for Tecumseh. For one, it had made him even more determined. "I stood upon the ashes of my own home," Tecumseh remembered, "and there I summoned the spirits of the

After the crushing defeat at Tippecanoe, Tecumseh banished Tenskwatawa from Prophetstown, thus ending his career as a prophet.

braves who had fallen in their vain attempt to protect their homes from the grasping invader, and as I sniffed up the smell of their blood from the ground I swore once more eternal hatred—the hatred of an avenger."[54] Now there was no choice. His people could not wait; they would have to start the war now.

A British colonel named Matthew Elliot, the superintendent of Indian affairs for Upper Canada, knew and respected Tecumseh and had believed that he could unite all the North American Indians. He had advised Tecumseh against rushing into open warfare. But, at the same time, he had supplied Tecumseh and his followers with weapons, blankets, and other necessities. Tecumseh knew that the defeat at Tippecanoe had erased much of what he had been trying to do over the past fifteen years. But it had made clear that the smartest thing he could do was offer his services and those of his warriors to the British.

All across Indiana, Ohio, and Michigan, Indian nations met in councils in the spring of 1812. Where the Wabash and the Mississippi met, so did the nations of the Northwest—Wyandot, Chippewa, Potawatomi, Miami, Delaware, Shawnee. At one council, Tecumseh defended himself and his people. "I challenge anyone," he said, "to say we ever advised anyone, directly or indirectly, to make war on our white brothers. . . . Governor Harrison made war on my people in my absence . . . had I been at home, there would have been no blood shed at that time."[55]

Two days after he spoke those words, Tecumseh set out for Fort Malden. With him rode around two hundred warriors from thirty-two Indian nations, including the Winnebago, the Ottawa, the Potawa-tomi, the Sioux, and the Sac and Fox. They went first to Fort Wayne, from there to the island of Bois Blanc in the Detroit River, then on to Ontario to Fort Malden. When they finally arrived at the fort, they made camp outside the wooden stockade. As they sat there, waiting for the war Tecumseh knew would soon come, he saw in his mind fifty thousand mounted warriors in battle.

Declaration of War

On June 18, 1812, the United States declared war on Great Britain. The declaration was due in great part to some American congressmen known as War Hawks, most of them from western and southern states. Among their leaders were South Carolinian John C. Calhoun, whose mother had been scalped by Cherokees; Tennessean Felix Grundy, who had lost three brothers in Indian raids; and Kentuckian Henry Clay, who believed that westward expansion was essential for the United States.

The War Hawks thought that the government should be doing more about the threat posed by the Indians in general and by Tecumseh in particular. They were sure that the British were helping Tecumseh and his followers and had been behind the attack on the U.S. Army. So long as Canada was a British colony, they argued, the Indians in North America would always have a power base. For several years, the War Hawks had pushed for the United States to go to war with Great Britain and invade Canada. Finally they convinced Congress that there was no other way for the two countries to come to terms.

Tecumseh in 1812

In 1812 Colonel W. S. Hatch of Cincinnati, who knew Tecumseh, saw him in the streets of Detroit. In a book he wrote, quoted in The Heroes of Defeat, *Hatch described the Shawnee leader as he was that day.*

"The personal appearance of this remarkable man was uncommonly fine. His height was about five feet nine inches, judging by my own height when standing close to him [corroborated by the late Colonel Johnson, for many years Indian agent at Piqua]; his face oval rather than angular; his nose handsome and straight; his mouth beautifully formed like that of Napoleon I, as represented in his portraits; his eyes clear, transparent hazel, with a mild, pleasant expression when in repose, or in conversation; but when excited in his orations, or by the enthusiasm of conflict, or when in anger, they appeared like balls of fire; his teeth beautifully white, and his complexion more of a light brown or tan than red; his arms and hands are beautifully formed; his limbs straight. He always stood very erect and walked with a brisk, elastic, vigorous step; invariably dressed in Indian-tanned buckskin; a perfectly well-fitting hunting frock, descending to the knee, was over his under clothes of the same material; the usual cape and finish of leather fringe about the neck, cape edges of the front opening and bottom of the frock; a belt of the same material, in which were his side-arms (an elegant silver mounted tomahawk and a knife in a strong leather case), short pantaloons, connected with neatly fitting leggings and moccasins, with a mantle of the same material thrown over his left shoulder, used as a blanket in camp, and as a protection in storm. Such was his dress when I last saw him on the 17th of August, 1812, on the streets of Detroit, mutually exchanging tokens of recognition with former acquaintances in times of peace, and pressing on, he to see that his Indians had all crossed to Malden, as commanded, and to counsel with his allies in regard to the next movement of the now really commenced war of 1812. He was then in the prime of life and presented in his appearance and noble bearing one of the finest looking men I have ever seen."

British and American soldiers engage in hand-to-hand combat during the War of 1812. For Tecumseh, the war symbolized his people's last hope for halting the American invasion.

As soon as war was declared, both the British and the Americans tried to get backing from the Indian nations. Tecumseh saw the war as a last chance for his people to stop American settlers from taking their land. At one point, he told a Wyandot chief friendly with the Americans,

> Here is a chance, a chance such as will never occur again: for us Indians of North America to form ourselves into one great combination and cast our lot with the British in this war. And should they conquer and again get the mastery of all North America, our rights to at least a portion of the land of our fathers would be respected by the King. If they should not win and the whole country should pass into the hands of the Long Knives—we see this plainly—it will not be many years before our last place of abode and our last hunting ground will be taken from us, and the remnants of the different tribes between the Mississippi, the Lakes, and the Ohio River will all be driven toward the setting sun.[56]

The Wyandot chief Tecumseh had tried to convince did not join the British. But he did not join the Americans either. Instead, he insisted that his village stay neutral.

During the three years the war raged, thousands of warriors and their families camped on the Canadian bank of the Detroit River. Conditions were harsh. Because the Indians were unused to measuring out their rationed food, and the British did not always have enough for everyone, before the war was over, many had died from malnutrition. Many others froze to death.

An American Invasion

Not long after the Americans declared war on the British, Brigadier General William Hull, governor of the Michigan Territory, set out to locate Tecumseh and find out exactly what he was doing. Hull was sixty years old. Someone who knew him described him as a "short, corpulent [overweight], good-natured, old gentleman who bore the marks of good eating and drinking."[57]

Hull had heard that Tecumseh and the commander of Fort Malden were close allies who met every day. Hull had no way of knowing how wrong his information was. In July he and an army of several thousand pushed north from Detroit to invade Canada. Tecumseh and his warriors crossed the river and did their best to stop them. During the fighting, Tecumseh was wounded in the leg. Hull's troops proved to be too many and too strong. They pushed the British, and with them their Indian allies, back into Canada.

A Friend at Fort Malden

On August 13, 1812, a professional soldier who was also a Canadian governor took command of Fort Malden. Forty-three-year-old Major General Isaac Brock, over six feet tall, with blonde hair and blue eyes, was nothing like Tecumseh in ap-

General William Hull, the aged commander of Fort Detroit, forced Tecumseh and his warriors to retreat to Canada and the safety of Fort Malden.

pearance. But in personality and spirit, the two men were very similar. Both were bold, full of energy, strong willed, and self-confident. Both were cared about and highly regarded by their men. Brock knew that tiny Fort Malden, with its few rickety wooden buildings, could not be defended against thousands of U.S. troops.

The British ministry had warned Brock not to encourage the Indians of the Northwest Territory in their raids on the Americans. So he knew of Tecumseh before arriving at Fort Malden. The night Brock took command of the fort, he met with the Shawnee he had heard so much about. Tecumseh appeared for the meeting dressed in a buckskin jacket and leggings, moccasins decorated with brightly colored porcupine quills, a single feather in his shining black hair, and three coins hanging from his nose.

Attack Fort Detroit, Tecumseh advised Brock. When Brock reminded him that there were three thousand men at Fort Detroit, Tecumseh explained that General William Hull, who commanded the fort, would not put up a fight if taken by surprise. Hull had not wanted the command at all, and when he asked to be replaced, President Madison, who had talked him into taking the post in the first place, had convinced him to stay. Hull, Tecumseh said, was scared to death of the thought of an Indian massacre. Kneeling on the ground in front of Brock, Tecumseh used the point of his hunting knife to draw on a piece of bark a map of Fort Detroit, complete with streams and forest paths. He described with great care the fort's defenses, not the least of which was the high log stockade—the tops carved to

General Hull at Sandwich

In 1812 the American general William Hull invaded Canada. As he and his troops pulled their weapons of war through the streets of Sandwich, a town on the Canadian side of the Detroit River, the general offered these words to Canadians. The quote is taken from Tecumseh: Fact and Fiction in Early Records.

"Inhabitants of Canada! After thirty years of Peace and prosperity the United States have been driven to Arms. The injuries and aggressions, the insults and indignities of Great Britain have *once more* left them no alternative but manly resistance. . . . The army under my Command has invaded your Country and the standard of the United States waves on the territory of Canada. To the peaceful unoffending inhabitant, It brings neither danger nor difficulty. I come to *find* enemies not to *make* them, I come to protect not to *injure* you. . . .

If the barbarous and Savage policy of Great Britain be pursued, and the savages are let loose to murder our Citizens and butcher our women and children, this war, will be a war of extermination.

The first stroke with the Tomahawk, the first attempt with the Scalping Knife will be the Signal for one indiscriminate [unrestrained] scene of desolation. *No white man found fighting by the Side of an Indian will be taken prisoner.* Instant destruction will be his Lot. . . .

I doubt not your courage and firmness; I will not doubt your attachment to Liberty. If you tender your services voluntarily they will be accepted readily.

The United States offer you *Peace, Liberty,* and *Security,* your choice lies between these, & *War, Slavery,* and *destruction.* Choose them, but choose wisely."

sharp points—that surrounded the fort and the town.

British officers tried to talk Brock out of listening to Tecumseh's plan. But Brock paid no attention. He liked—and trusted—Tecumseh. He told the Shawnee leader that if his men captured the fort, he personally would do all he could to help the Indians get back their land. Tecumseh's bitterness showed as he told Brock how he felt about the Americans:

> The Americans are our enemies. They came to us hungry and they cut off the hands of our brothers who gave them corn. We gave them rivers of fish, and they poisoned our fountains. We gave them forest-clad mountains and valleys full of game, and in return what did they give our warriors and our women? Whiskey and trinkets and a grave![58]

The next day Brock, Tecumseh, and their armies headed north. Brock made Tecumseh a brigadier general and gave him full charge of the Indian forces. The Indian Department provided advisers to help with the several thousand Indians who had gathered to form Tecumseh's confederacy, the one he had dreamed about for so long. Tecumseh's warriors dressed in loincloths and moccasins, and their hair, shiny with bear grease, stood up in spikes. To bring good magic to protect themselves and to help them blend into the forest's dim light and moving shadows, they had painted their bodies with brightly colored and strange patterns.

The Taking of Detroit

Tecumseh and his warriors, scalping knives clasped between their teeth, silently slipped into the waters of the Detroit River. Soon they surfaced on the other bank, dripping water and armed with muskets, spears, bows and arrows, and tomahawks. They surrounded Detroit, cutting it off from land contact with the outside world. Brock, meanwhile, had sent out a British messenger with instructions to let himself be captured. Once in the presence of American officers, the messenger was to say that Tecumseh and five thousand warriors were on the way, eager to fight. In fact, Tecumseh had only six hundred warriors. But by running back and forth in the woods, screaming and shouting, they created the illusion of being a great army.

Tecumseh and British general Isaac Brock (pictured) joined forces to defeat the Americans. Brock, who considered Tecumseh a "gallant warrior," made the Shawnee chieftain a brigadier general in the British military.

General Hull formally surrenders Fort Detroit and his twenty-five-hundred-man force to General Brock; the surrender of Detroit was the only time in U.S. history that an American city succumbed to a foreign power.

The tactic worked. Hull thought that thousands of wild savages were in the woods, preparing to storm his fort. Without even checking with his officers, he put out a white flag and surrendered his force of twenty-five hundred men. It was the first and only time an American city ever surrendered to a foreign country. One author wrote:

On the 17th of August, the success of the British, which even they did not call a victory, was celebrated. They had recovered at this surrender some British cannon taken during the Revolutionary War. These pieces were welcomed with joy and even kisses by the British officers. The recaptured cannon were fired at the British celebration, and their fire was answered by the English war vessel "Queen Charlotte," which was much admired by the Western soldiers, being the first they had seen.[59]

Most of Hull's officers had been angry when he surrendered. Some had even cried. Settlers in Ohio, Indiana, and Kentucky did not like what Hull had done either. The aging general was court-martialed for cowardice and sentenced to hang, but President Madison pardoned him.

Proud and defiant with victory, Tecumseh marched into Detroit. On his head was a red cap topped with one white-tipped eagle feather. His breechcloth was blue and his fringed buckskin leggings red. On his feet were buckskin moccasins.

To show his respect for his British allies, he draped around his shoulders a coat like those British generals wore. From his neck hung a silver medal. To make sure that his braves did not abuse any civilian living in Detroit, he warned them that the penalty for torturing, murdering, raping, or stealing from civilians was death.

Brock knew that he owed this victory to Tecumseh. The Shawnee, said Brock, was a "gallant warrior."[60] To show his respect and friendship, Brock gave Tecumseh his own silk officer's sash, a pair of pistols, and an engraved compass. In return, Tecumseh offered Brock a beaded belt, which Brock kept for the rest of his life. When Brock saw Tecumseh the next day, he was not wearing the sash. Puzzled, Brock asked what had happened to it. Tecumseh, who had very little respect or use for whites, then paid Brock a great compliment. He could not wear such a mark of distinction, he said, when an older and more skilled warrior was present. So he had given the sash to his lieutenant, the Wyandot chief Roundhead.

When Brock moved his headquarters to a house in Detroit, he told Tecumseh that the house was his home too. As proof, he gave Tecumseh his own parlor and bedroom. In his report about the surrender of Fort Detroit, Brock wrote, "Among all the Indians I found at Malden who had arrived from various parts of the country, there was one of extraordinary qualities. He was the Shawnee Chieftain, Tecumseh. A more sagacious [wise] man or a more gallant warrior does not exist. He was the admiration of every one who conversed with him."[61] In the same report, quoted in a different source, Brock stated that under Tecumseh's leadership, "the instant the enemy submitted, his life became sacred."[62]

A New Commander

Brock soon was sent to stop an American attack at the border at Niagara, and Colonel Henry Proctor arrived to take his place. No two men could have been more different. Brock thought first about his men and his duty. Proctor thought first about Proctor. Brock respected the Indians of North America. Proctor hated them. He did not like Canadians much either. Brock was bright and quick. Proctor was dull and slow. Brock was a great leader and honest. Proctor was unfit and dishonest. Tecumseh disliked Proctor from the first.

One of the first things Proctor did when he took command was to order every American in Detroit to swear loyalty to the British Crown. Among those who

Henry Proctor (pictured) and his predecessor, Isaac Brock, could not have been more different. Tecumseh disliked Proctor from the beginning, considering him to be dishonest and selfish.

refused was a priest named Father Gabril, a friend to the Indians. "I have taken one oath to support the Constitution of the United States," he declared, "and I cannot take another. Do with me as you please."[63] Proctor put him in prison. Tecumseh demanded that Proctor let the priest go. Proctor gave in, but the incident only made him hate—and fear—Tecumseh even more than before.

In September 1812, Tecumseh went south to urge the Creeks to make war in that part of the country. A month later, he returned to Fort Malden with about three thousand warriors. It was the largest army ever brought together by the Indians. Bad news greeted him: Brock was dead, killed in battle. Tecumseh also was not pleased to hear that Proctor was now a general, in charge of troops in Upper Canada, and commander of Fort Malden.

Massacre at River Raisin

In January 1813 Kentucky troops forced the British at Frenchtown on the River Raisin to withdraw south of Detroit to Brownstown. The Kentuckians, all 850 of them, decided to make camp at Frenchtown. Before they could react, Proctor, with help from Roundhead's warriors and 30 of Little Warrior's Upper Creeks, attacked, capturing and killing almost everyone. Proctor promised to protect the wounded Kentuckians if they surrendered. Instead, he allowed the warriors, many of them drunk, to scalp the Americans as they lay helpless in the snow. Kentuckians blamed Tecumseh for what had happened and made "Remember the River Raisin" their battle cry.

Meanwhile, Proctor's Creek allies headed back home. Near the mouth of the Ohio River, they murdered some white settlers. Neither the Upper nor the Lower Creeks could decide what to do about the killings. Therefore, a council of Creek elders stepped in. Its decision—to have Little Warrior and his followers captured and executed—provoked a bitter and bloody civil war between Creeks.

Attack on Fort Meigs

In February 1813 William Henry Harrison built a small fort high on a bluff above the Maumee River, not far from the site of the Battle of Fallen Timbers. Called Fort Meigs, it was to be Harrison's headquarters until he was ready to take back Detroit.

Two months later, Proctor and Tecumseh led a British attack on the fort. It had taken Tecumseh that long to get Proctor to move. Tecumseh sent Harrison a message:

> "I have come with eight hundred braves," he lied. "You have an equal number in your hiding place. Come out with them and give me a battle. You talked like a brave man when we met at Vincennes, and I respected you, but now you hide between logs and in the earth, like a ground hog. Give me your answer."[64]

But Harrison did not answer. For eight days Tecumseh and the British laid siege to the fort, but the British general hesitated to move in for the capture. This gave the defenders time to send for help, and in response, on May 5 about twelve hundred Kentucky militiamen came down the river above the fort. No one had been watching the river, so Proctor was taken by surprise. The Kentuckians were not disciplined soldiers, however, and their helter-skelter charge gave the British troops and Tecumseh's warriors the opening they needed. Before the Kentuckians knew what had hit them, they were surrounded. Soon close to 500 Kentuckians lay dead, and another 150 were prisoners.

Tecumseh wanted Proctor to return to the fort and force Harrison to surrender, pointing out that otherwise the Americans would be able to rebuild their strength. But Proctor would not listen. He marched his men and the prisoners back to Fort Malden. Tecumseh stayed behind at Meigs to keep watch. Upon arrival at the British headquarters, the prisoners were forced to run naked between two lines of warriors, who attacked them with war clubs, tomahawks, and knives. Proctor did nothing to stop the slaughter. Finally a disgusted British officer sent for Tecumseh, begging him to return right away.

By the time Tecumseh arrived, more than twenty prisoners had been tomahawked or beaten to death and scalped. The ones still alive were in shock. A group of warriors surrounded one prisoner while a brave stood with his tomahawk raised over him. Furious, Tecumseh charged, riding straight at the guilty brave. An eyewitness, a British colonel, said "he was the maddest looking man I ever saw, his eyes shot fire, he was terrible."[65] As soon as he got close enough, he grabbed a knife from one warrior. With his other hand, using the flat side of his sword, he hit another warrior on the head so hard that he fell to the ground. Tecumseh jumped off his horse and stood between the warriors and the prisoners. Grabbing one warrior, he slapped him—hard. "Are there no men here?"[66] he asked sadly. Why, he wondered, could his people not control their anger?

Next Tecumseh went to face Proctor. He wanted to know why the commanding officer had stood by and let such injustice and

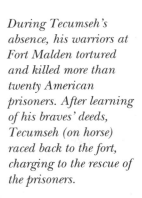

During Tecumseh's absence, his warriors at Fort Malden tortured and killed more than twenty American prisoners. After learning of his braves' deeds, Tecumseh (on horse) raced back to the fort, charging to the rescue of the prisoners.

cruelty take place. When Proctor replied that the warriors could not be commanded or controlled, Tecumseh lost his temper. He called Proctor all kinds of names and insulted him. "Be gone!" he screamed at Proctor. "I conquer to save, and you to murder. You are unfit to command."[67] An insult reported by another writer was "go and put on petticoats!"[68] Proctor got even by ordering that the Indians be fed horsemeat instead of beef. But when Tecumseh threatened to fight him one on one, Proctor quickly reversed the order.

The Beginning of the End

While the Americans were battling Proctor and his allies, an American naval commander named Oliver Hazard Perry had been building a fleet that could be used to break the British navy's stronghold on Lake Erie. On September 10, 1813, Perry took on the British and won. In one of the most famous military dispatches in American history, he passed the news to Harrison with the words: "We have met the enemy, and they are ours." Perry's victory was complete. He had destroyed the English fleet on Lake Erie, cutting off the British supply lines to Fort Malden. When Proctor heard of Perry's victory, he panicked. He was afraid that if he told Tecumseh what had happened, the Shawnee and his warriors would leave. But Tecumseh already knew, and the British defeat only made him more determined not to give in. Proctor, meanwhile, made secret plans to retreat from Detroit.

About a week later, Proctor called together his officers, told them to abandon Detroit, and ordered the burning of the

Tecumseh reprimands General Proctor for his failure to restrain the Indians from torturing the Americans. "I conquer to save, and you to murder. You are unfit for command," Tecumseh furiously informed Proctor.

main base and all the supplies at Fort Malden. The enemy, said Proctor, outnumbered them. And while they were low on food and guns, the Americans had plenty of both. The only thing they could do, he said, was to burn their forts so that the Americans would find nothing but ashes. Quickly Tecumseh called together his followers. Of the fourteen thousand at the fort, his warriors and their families accounted for nearly three-quarters. They did not want to run away from Harrison. Neither did many of the British soldiers to whom Tecumseh spoke these words:

A Plea to Proctor

As Benjamin Drake, for many years the chief biographer of Tecumseh, reports in The Life of Tecumseh and of His Brother The Prophet, *when Tecumseh learned that Henry Proctor, the British general, was going to burn Fort Malden and retreat from the Americans, he lobbied strenuously for a change of plans.*

"Father, listen to your children! You have them now all before you.

The war before this [the American Revolution], our British father [the king] gave the hatchet to his red children, when our old chiefs were alive. They are now dead. In that war our father was thrown on his back by the Americans; and our father took them by the hand without our knowledge; and we are afraid that our father will do so again at this time.

Listen! when war was declared, our father stood up and gave us the tomahawk, and told us that he was then ready to strike the Americans; that he wanted our assistance, and that he would get our lands back, which the Americans have taken from us.

Father, listen! our fleet has gone out; we know they have fought; we have heard the great guns; . . . Our ships have gone one way, and we are much astonished to see our father tying up everything and preparing to run away the other, without letting his red children know what his intentions are. You always told us to remain here and take care of our lands; it made our hearts glad to hear that was your wish. Our great father, the king, is the head, and you represent him. You always told us you would never draw your foot off British ground; but now, father, we see that you are drawing back, and we are sorry to see our father doing so without seeing the enemy. We must compare our father's conduct to a fat dog that carries its tail on its back, but when affrighted, drops it between its legs and runs off.

Father, listen! the Americans have not yet defeated us by land; neither are we sure that they have done so by water; *we, therefore, wish to remain here and fight our enemy, should they make their appearance.* If they defeat us, we will then retreat with our father."

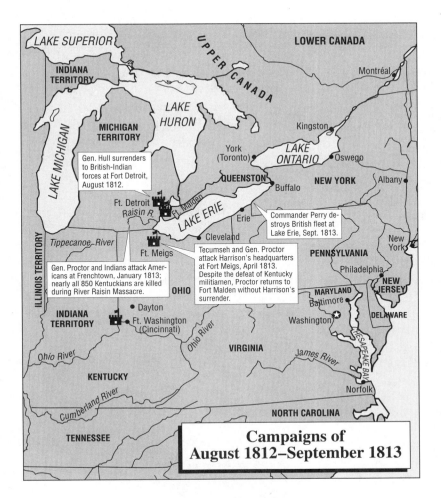

**Campaigns of
August 1812–September 1813**

Map labels:
LAKE SUPERIOR · LOWER CANADA · INDIANA TERRITORY · UPPER CANADA · Montréal · MICHIGAN TERRITORY · LAKE HURON · LAKE MICHIGAN · Kingston · York (Toronto) · LAKE ONTARIO · Oswego · QUEENSTON · Buffalo · NEW YORK · Albany · Ft. Detroit · Ft. Malden · Raisin R. · LAKE ERIE · Erie · Cleveland · New York · Ft. Meigs · PENNSYLVANIA · Philadelphia · Tippecanoe River · ILLINOIS TERRITORY · OHIO · NEW JERSEY · Dayton · MARYLAND · Baltimore · DELAWARE · INDIANA TERRITORY · Ft. Washington (Cincinnati) · Washington · Ohio River · VIRGINIA · James River · CHESAPEAKE BAY · Ohio River · KENTUCKY · Cumberland River · Norfolk · NORTH CAROLINA · TENNESSEE

Gen. Hull surrenders to British-Indian forces at Fort Detroit, August 1812.

Commander Perry destroys British fleet at Lake Erie, Sept. 1813.

Tecumseh and Gen. Proctor attack Harrison's headquarters at Fort Meigs, April 1813. Despite the defeat of Kentucky militiamen, Proctor returns to Fort Malden without Harrison's surrender.

Gen. Proctor and Indians attack Americans at Frenchtown, January 1813; nearly all 850 Kentuckians are killed during River Raisin Massacre.

"I speak in the names of the Indian chiefs and warriors to General Proctor as the representative of the great father, the King," said Tecumseh with much feeling. "You have arms and ammunition which our great father sent for his red children. If you have an idea of going away, give them to us, and you may go and [are] welcome [to do so]. Our lives are in the hands of the Great Spirit. He gave to our ancestors the lands which we possess. We are determined to defend them, and if it be His will, our bones will whiten on them, but we will never give up."[69]

One of the men who witnessed the speech said that "the darkness" of Tecumseh's complexion "and the brilliancy of his [dark] and piercing eye gave a singularly wild and terrific expression to his features. It was evident that he could be terrible."[70]

Tecumseh's speech was long and moving, almost a plea. But Proctor paid no attention. He was going to burn the fort. Tecumseh had no choice but to organize his people and follow the retreating British soldiers up the Thames River.

8 Tecumseh's Last Prophecy: "The Touch of Death"

Tecumseh had made it clear that even if General Proctor was willing to give up, he and his braves were not. They were determined to fight to the bitter end. For Tecumseh, the decision to fight would be a fatal one—both for him personally and for his dream.

I Shall Not Return

On October 4, 1813, Tecumseh learned that his old enemy William Henry Harrison and a big army of Americans were nearing the Thames River. Suddenly Tecumseh and some of the British officers heard what sounded like a shot. Tecumseh doubled over as if hit by a bullet. But there had been no shot, and there was no bullet. A strange look came into Tecumseh's eyes. Now he knew. He told the officers that a bad spirit was there with them: "Brother warriors," he said, "we are about to enter an engagement from which I shall never come out—my body will remain on the field of battle." No one argued. All was silent. Then Tecumseh unbuckled his sword and handed it to one of his warriors, saying these words: "When my son becomes a noted warrior, and able to wield a sword, give this to him."[71]

Then Tecumseh dressed for battle. He took off the red British coat and put on buckskins. He painted his face red with the paint of war. Telling Proctor that he would fight with or without him, Tecumseh explained his battle plan. Later, a British soldier described the scene this way:

In Tecumseh's final prophecy, he envisioned his own death on the battlefield. With this knowledge, Tecumseh prepared himself and his warriors for what would prove to be his last battle.

Tecumseh, the Man

More than fifty years ago, Lloyd Emerson Siberell, a historian and author who did much research on Tecumseh, described the Shawnee this way in his reminiscences of the great chief.

"Very striking in appearance and manner, Tecumseh possessed a lithe, light, and finely proportioned figure, and an expressive face, oval in shape and somewhat angular. Unlike the usual Indian, his eyes were a hazel color—well spaced, clear, and lively. . . . His complexion was a light tan or brown. From his nose were suspended three crosses or coronets made of silver.

His usual costume consisted of a well fitted tanned buckskin hunting shirt or jacket with neatly cut fringe and trousers of the same material. On his feet were moccasins, ornamented with dyed porcupine quills. His head-dress usually consisted of a red cap with a band of quills and a single eagle feather that was black with a white tip.

His only ornament was a large silver medallion of King George III. . . . This was attached to a varicolored wampum string and suspended from his neck. . . .

Honesty and fearlessness were two of his outstanding qualities. To this was added a tradition of leadership and a certain austerity [strictness] of manner without which he could never have controlled his wayward followers. A typical member of this race, he shared its quality of silence, but when aroused he could be both forceful and persuasive. His fame as an orator became almost as great as his skill as a hunter and warrior. An ideal Indian, he possesses a fine memory and physique, a profound contempt for hypocrisy, and a complete knowledge of the ways of the forest and battle. To all white men with whom Tecumseh came in contact, he appealed strongly as a man of courage and integrity."

Only a few minutes before the clang of the American bugles was heard ringing through the forest, the haughty chieftain had passed along our line, pleased with the manner in which his left was supported, and seemingly sanguine of success [optimistic]. He was dressed in his usual deer skin dress, which admirably displayed his light yet sinewy figure, and in his handkerchief, rolled as a turban over his brow, was placed a handsome white ostrich feather . . . on which he was ever fond of decorating himself, either for the Hall of Council or the battle field. He pressed the hand of each officer as he passed, made some remark in Shawnee appropriate to the occasion, which was sufficiently understood by the expressive signs accompanying them, and then passed away forever from our view.[72]

The next day, the fleeing Proctor was left no choice but to turn and defend himself. To his left was a high bank that would help keep the Americans from coming along the side of them or attacking from behind. To the right was a small swamp that turned into a larger one. Tecumseh and his braves formed a line that curved from one swamp to the other. Tecumseh knew they were outnumbered—almost three to one.

Late in the afternoon, Harrison's cavalry of Kentuckians charged. The air was filled with the sounds of clattering horses' hooves, bugles, and cries of "Remember the River Raisin!" General Proctor was terrified. He made a dash for the carriage he had waiting and took off for eastern Ontario, where he would be safe. When he fled, he left behind six hundred soldiers. Surrounded by Americans, their leader gone, the British troops surrendered without ever firing their artillery. Later Proctor was brought before a military court, which gave him a bad scolding. He returned to England and lived to an old age.

Tecumseh and his braves, prepared to fight to the death, did not give up so easily. Colonel Richard M. Johnson's Kentucky cavalry attacked. Not until Johnson's

men reached the edge of the marsh did Tecumseh's warriors let loose their fire. All the Kentuckians but Johnson got off their horses and advanced slowly on foot into the marsh to face Tecumseh's braves.

Tecumseh, who had been hurt in an earlier battle and wore a bandage on his arm, was wounded again and again. Blood from a head wound ran down his face. Blood poured from his mouth. A big red spot was spreading on his buckskin shirt where a bullet had entered his chest. But still he kept on fighting—reloading and firing, encouraging his braves to fight on. "He yelled like a tiger," said an American soldier, "and urged his braves to attack."[73] Hand to hand, face to face, Indian and Kentuckian kept fighting. With only their tomahawks left, Tecumseh's braves still did not give up—until the voice of their leader was heard no more. Tecumseh's prophecy had come to pass.

The Death of Tecumseh

The battle was over, and bodies—white and red—littered the landscape. But which body was Tecumseh's? And who had killed him?

A British officer found a mutilated body that he and some other officers said was Tecumseh's. The body had been scalped, and long strips of skin had been torn from the back and the thighs. But years later some of Tecumseh's followers claimed that the body had not been Tecumseh's. Naw Naw, Shabbona, Black Hawk, Noonday, and others told how

in the dead of night Tecumseh's faithful little band went over the battlefield examining the bodies until they found the chief's. A bullet had passed through his heart. His skull had been crushed by a gun butt. Otherwise his body was not mutilated. They lifted it carefully and carried it four or five miles away before they buried it in an unmarked grave.[74]

An American officer said he had seen Tecumseh before it got dark. He was sure it was Tecumseh because he had a bandaged arm. "There was something so majestic, so dignified, and yet so mild, in his countenance as he lay stretched on the ground," said the American officer, "where a few minutes before he rallied his men to the fight, that while gazing on him with admiration and pity, I forgot he was a savage."[75]

Maybe Tecumseh was killed by a sixty-four-year-old American colonel named William Whitley. He and Tecumseh might have exchanged fatal shots at the same moment. Or maybe a Kentuckian, Colonel Richard Johnson, killed Tecumseh. Johnson, even though he had been wounded twice, led the cavalry charge into the marsh on horseback. He stayed on his horse until an Indian dressed in light buckskin stood right in front of him and shot him in the arm. Johnson then shot the warrior in the face and the warrior fell over, dead. Almost instantly, the rest of the braves stopped fighting and dropped back into the shadows of the forest as if they had received a signal. Even though Johnson swore he had killed Tecumseh, the warrior he shot was much larger, taller,

Tecumseh (left) falls backwards to his death in this reconstruction of the Battle of Thames. Although many stories exist about Tecumseh's final moments, the identity of his assailant remains a mystery.

Tecumseh collapses from a gun-shot wound during the grisly Battle of Thames. After the great Shawnee leader fell silent, his braves were forced to retreat.

and darker than Tecumseh. And his eyes were black, not hazel.

Then there is the story a Potawatomi chief told when he was asked by Indian affairs superintendent William Clark what he remembered about the day Tecumseh was killed:

"Were you at the battle of the Thames?," the agent asked. "Yes," said the chief. "Did you know Tecumseh?," asked the agent. "Yes," said the chief.

"Were you near him in the fight?," inquired the agent. "Yes," responded the chief. "Did you see him fall?," the agent queried. "Yes," the chief replied. "Who shot him," asked the agent. "Don't know," said the chief. "Did you see the man that shot him?" the agent wanted to know. "Yes," replied the chief. "What sort of looking man was he?," the agent questioned. "Short, thick man," replied the American Indian. "What color was the horse he rode?," the agent asked. "Most white," answered the chief. "How do you know this man shot Tecumseh?," said the agent. The chief thought for a moment and then replied, "I saw the man ride up—saw his horse get tangled in some bushes—when the horse was most still, I saw Tecumseh level his rifle at the man and shoot—the man shook on his horse—soon the horse got out of the bushes, and the man spurred him up—horse came slow—Tecumseh right before him—man's left hand hung down—just as he got near, Tecumseh lifted his tomahawk and was going to throw it, when the man shot him with a shot gun—Tecumseh fell dead and we all ran."[76]

A Tribute to Tecumseh

This tribute to Tecumseh appears in The Indian Tribes of Ohio Historically Considered. *It was written in the late 1800s, a time when most whites looked on Native Americans as savages whose civilization was inferior to that of the Europeans.*

"As time passes, . . . we can safely place Tecumtha above all the other actors in that drama. I am persuaded that none of them approached him in courage and natural ability. We must remember that Tecumtha was reared among savages. That he should possess intelligence, humanity and all the qualities of a great leader and exhibit fine traits of character is surprising. We naturally expect such in the nature of those who have dwelt under the protection and culture of civilization. In view of his disadvantages and that he successfully coped with them, elevating himself among the great men of his time irrespective of color, he is deserving of highest honor.

Tecumtha died as he lived—facing the foe. A more heroic, dauntless and determined character is not to be found on the pages of history in any land or of any time. He had but a few hundred men; thousands were hurled against him. He could never hope for success, but he hesitated not. He came of a noble tribe, one 'whose business was war,' and it reverenced him. During these troublesome times he was as a rock jutting out of the sea against which the waves beat and raged in vain. He was a Colossus [giant], towering above other men, representing all that was highest and best in the native Americans. His name is assured undying fame and his deeds will live as long as there is a history of America."

As far as anyone knows, no white man saw Tecumseh die. But even if one had, Tecumseh was dressed exactly like all of the other warriors, so unless the white had actually seen or known Tecumseh before, there was no way to tell him from any other Indian on the battlefield. The warriors near Tecumseh when he died—sometime during the last twenty minutes of the fight—said they did not know who killed him.

The Burial Place of a Warrior

Everyone knows where Tecumseh died, but only the Shawnee know where he is buried. According to one of his relatives, Tecumseh "fell in the thick of the fight," but his body was retrieved by his warriors and taken to a point well marked on the banks of a creek some five miles away and buried there. Several years later, a band of Shawnees who knew the spot traveled there to retrieve the remains and carry them to their western reservation. They found that the creek at flood time had washed away all evidence of the great warrior's resting place.

An Indian chief named Sha-wah-wan-noo on St. Anne's Island preserved a set of bones that he said were Tecumseh's. When the remains were examined, the thigh bone did not show any sign of a fracture. In time the bones ended up at Walpole Island, in Ontario, and were buried there. A monument to Tecumseh was built over the burial place.

The Death of a Dream

At Wapakoneta, Tecumseh had said that his cause would live on after he died. But, for once, he was wrong. When he died, his dream died with him. Without him as a leader, his followers became frustrated. They stopped working to unite their people into one great nation. The Prophet was right when years later he said, "Tecumseh was a great general, and nothing but his premature death defeated his grand plan."[77]

Some of the people closest to Tecumseh turned to Tenskwatawa to lead them. And they gave Tecumseh's son the status of village chief. But neither man was the leader the people wanted—or needed. The words of an Ottawa chief named Naibush rang all too true. "Since our great chief Tecumtha has been killed," Naibush lamented, "we do not listen to one another, we do not rise together, we hurt ourselves by it, it is our own fault . . . we do not when we go to war rise together, but we go one or two and the rest say they will go tomorrow."[78]

The War of 1812—the war that ended the life of Tecumseh—was a turning point in U.S. history. Some people called it the "Second War of Independence." The Battle of the Thames and the death of Tecumseh signaled the end of the political, social, and military unity of the Indians of the Northwest. One of the most powerful leaders of the North American Indians was dead. Once again the United States had control of the Northwest Territory. And the British were forced to admit that the region was not a set of colonies but a true and independent nation. Whites kept coming and overrunning Indian land. The Shawnee and other Indian nations were forced farther and farther west. In time, some groups of Shawnee settled in Oklahoma. Before too many years went by, the Indians, broken and scattered, were made to live on small reservations by the government of the whites who had taken their lands.

When Tecumseh died, his dream of uniting the northwestern Indians died along with him. The North American Indians scattered and were finally forced to live on government reservations (pictured).

The dream died, but the legend of Tecumseh did not. In 1837, Richard Johnson ran for political office and used the rumor that he had killed Tecumseh as a campaign slogan: "Rumpsey, Dumpsey, Colonel Johnson killed Tecumseh."[79] Johnson served as vice president of the United States in the administration of Martin Van Buren. As time passed, more whites came to admire Tecumseh for his bravery and his high ideals. The famous Civil War general William Tecumseh Sherman was named after the great Shawnee. Towns and street signs—even a mountaintop in New England—bear his name today.

Like the Americans he fought against, Tecumseh believed in courage, honor, and freedom. In 1860 an Indiana newspaper paid the Shawnee leader great tribute. "Tecumseh was a great man," said the reporter. "He was truly great—and his greatness was his own, unassisted by science or the aids of education. As a statesman, a warrior, and a patriot, we shall not look upon his like again."[80] But the greatest tribute of all is that stated by Shawnee tradition:

No white man knows, or ever will know, where we took the body of our beloved Tecumseh and buried him. Tecumseh will come again!

Notes

Introduction: "I Shall Stamp on the Ground with My Foot"

1. William Atkinson, *The Next New Madrid Earthquake: A Survival Guide for the Midwest*. Carbondale and Edwardsville: Southern Illinois University Press, 1989, pp. 9–11.

2. Thomas L. McKenney and James Hall, Esq., *History of the Indian Tribes of North America, with Biographical Sketches and Anecdotes of the Principal Chiefs*, vol. II. 1842. Reprint Kent, OH: Volair Limited, 1978, p. 62.

Chapter One: Night of the Panther Passing Over

3. Joseph Bryan Icenhower, *Tecumseh and the Indian Confederation, 1811–1813: The Indian Nations East of the Mississippi Are Defeated*. New York: Franklin Watts, 1975, p. 15.

4. Laura Pienkny Zakin, "The Passing of a People," *Columbus Monthly*, July 1993, p. 90.

5. Quoted in William Jackson Armstrong, *The Heroes of Defeat*. Cincinnati, OH: Robert Clarke, 1905, p. 291.

6. Chuck Fulkerson, *Native American People: The Shawnee*. Vero Beach, FL: Rourke, 1992, p. 22.

7. Quoted in Armstrong, *The Heroes of Defeat*, pp. 302–303.

Chapter Two: From Boyhood to Manhood

8. Quoted in William H. Van Hoose, *Tecumseh: An Indian Moses*. Canton, OH: Daring Books, 1984, pp. 17–18.

9. Quoted in Allan W. Eckert, *A Sorrow in Our Heart: The Life of Tecumseh*. New York: Bantam Books, 1992, pp. 300–302.

10. Quoted in Eckert, *A Sorrow in Our Heart*, p. 318.

Chapter 3: Uniting a People

11. Elizabeth Eggleston Seelye, *Tecumseh and the Shawnee Prophet*. New York: Dodd, Mead, 1878, pp. 62–63.

12. John McDonald, "General Simon Kenton," *Biographical Sketches of General Nathaniel Massie, General Duncan McArthur, Captain William Wells, and General Simon Kenton*. Cincinnati, OH: E. Morgan, 1838, pp. 256–57.

13. Quoted in Eckert, *A Sorrow in Our Heart*, p. 375.

14. Quoted in Seelye, *Tecumseh and the Shawnee Prophet*, p. 87.

15. Quoted in Eckert, *A Sorrow in Our Heart*, p. 744.

16. Quoted in Jason Hook, *Tecumseh: Visionary Chief of the Shawnee*. Dorset, UK: Firebird Books, 1989, p. 18.

17. Quoted in Hook, *Tecumseh: Visionary Chief of the Shawnee*, p. 18.

18. Quoted in John Fleischman, "Tecumseh's New Take," *Ohio*, May 1994, p. 24.

Chapter 4: Family Ties

19. Eckert, *A Sorrow in Our Heart*, p. 426.

20. Quoted in R. David Edmunds, *The Shawnee Prophet*. Lincoln: University of Nebraska Press, 1983, p. 37.

21. Quoted in Carl Frederick Klinck, *Tecumseh: Fact and Fiction in Early Records*. Englewood Cliffs, NJ: Prentice-Hall, 1961, p. 36.

Chapter 5: This Land Is Ours

22. Quoted in Armstrong, *The Heroes of Defeat*, pp. 348–49.

23. Quoted in Armstrong, *The Heroes of Defeat*, pp. 333–34.

24. Quoted in Hook, *Tecumseh: Visionary Chief of the Shawnee*, p. 20.

25. Quoted in Eckert, *A Sorrow in Our Heart*, pp. 461–62.

26. Quoted in Benjamin Drake, *The Life of Tecumseh and of His Brother the Prophet; with a Historical Sketch of the Shawanoe Indians*, 1858. Reprint Salem, NH: Ayer, 1988, p. 90.

27. Quoted in Hook, *Tecumseh: Visionary Chief of the Shawnee*, p. 23.

28. Quoted in Luella Sanders Bruce Creighton, *Tecumseh: The Story of the Shawnee Chief*. Toronto: Macmillan, 1965, p. 69.

29. Quoted in Edmunds, *The Shawnee Prophet*, p. 62.

30. Quoted in Drake, *Life of Tecumseh and of His Brother the Prophet*, pp. 92–93.

Chapter 6: Endless Conflict

31. Quoted in Creighton, *Tecumseh: The Story of the Shawnee Chief*, p. 74.

32. Quoted in Creighton, *Tecumseh: The Story of the Shawnee Chief*, p. 74.

33. Quoted in Allan W. Eckert, *The Frontiersmen*. Boston: Little, Brown, 1967, p. 511.

34. Quoted in Kate Connell, *These Lands Are Ours: Tecumseh's Fight for the Old Northwest*. Austin, TX: Steck-Vaughn/Raintree, 1993, pp. 55–56.

35. Quoted in Connell, *These Lands Are Ours*, p. 56.

36. Quoted in Eckert, *A Sorrow in Our Heart*, p. 758.

37. Quoted in Creighton, *Tecumseh: Story of the Shawnee Chief*, p. 79.

38. Quoted in Hook, *Tecumseh: Visionary Chief of the Shawnee*, pp. 25–26.

39. Quoted in McKenney and Hall, *History of the Indian Tribes of North America*, p. 58.

40. Quoted in McKenney and Hall, *History of the Indian Tribes of North America*, p. 58.

41. Quoted in Eckert, *A Sorrow in Our Heart*, p. 762.

42. Quoted in Creighton, *Tecumseh: The Story of the Shawnee Chief*, p. 85.

43. Quoted in Creighton, *Tecumseh: The Story of the Shawnee Chief*, pp. 81–82.

44. Quoted in Lloyd Emerson Siberell, *Tecumseh: His Career, the Man, His Chillicothe Portrait*. Chillicothe, OH: Ross County Historical Society, 1944, pp. 6, 11.

45. Quoted in Klinck, *Tecumseh: Fact and Fiction in Early Records*, pp. 79–80.

46. Quoted in James McCague, *Tecumseh: Shawnee Warrior-Statesman*. Champaign, IL: Garrard, 1970, p. 54.

47. Quoted in Hook, *Tecumseh: Visionary Chief of the Shawnee*, p. 29.

48. Quoted in Ann McGovern, *The Defenders*. London: Scholastic Book Services, 1970, p. 72.

49. Quoted in McGovern, *The Defenders*, p. 72.

50. Quoted in Hook, *Tecumseh: Visionary Chief of the Shawnee*, p. 30.

51. Quoted in Drake, *The Life of Tecumseh and of His Brother the Prophet*, p. 152.

52. Quoted in McGovern, *The Defenders*, p. 74.

53. Quoted in Creighton, *Tecumseh: The Story of the Shawnee Chief*, p. 95.

Chapter 7: A New Alliance

54. Quoted in Hook, *Tecumseh: Visionary Chief of the Shawnee*, p. 32.

55. Quoted in Dumas Malone, ed., *Dictionary of American Biography*, vol. IX. New York: Charles Scribner's Sons, 1964, p. 360.

56. Quoted in Hook, *Tecumseh: Visionary Chief of the Shawnee*, p. 32.

57. Quoted in Robert Leckie, *The Wars of America*. New York: Harper & Row, 1968, p. 237.

58. Quoted in McGovern, *The Defenders*, p. 80.

59. Seelye, *Tecumseh and the Shawnee Prophet*, p. 247.

60. Quoted in Fulkerson, *Native American People: The Shawnee*, p. 24.

61. Quoted in Siberell, *Tecumseh*, p. 11.

62. Quoted in Icenhower, *Tecumseh and the Indian Confederation 1811–1813*, p. 62.

63. Quoted in McGovern, *The Defenders*, p. 83.

64. Quoted in Albert Marrin, *1812: The War Nobody Won*. New York: Atheneum, 1985, p. 38.

65. Quoted in Warren King Moorehead, *The Indian Tribes of Ohio Historically Considered: A Preliminary Paper*, 1899. Reprint, n.d., New York: AMS Press, for the Ohio State Archaeological and Historical Society by Fred J. Heer, p. 101.

66. Quoted in Marrin, *1812: The War Nobody Won*, p. 40.

67. Quoted in Marrin, *1812: The War Nobody Won*, p. 12.

68. Quoted in Hook, *Tecumseh: Visionary Chief of the Shawnee*, p. 36.

69. Quoted in Marrin, *1812: The War Nobody Won*, p. 98.

70. Quoted in Hook, *Tecumseh: Visionary Chief of the Shawnee*, p. 38.

Chapter 8: Tecumseh's Last Prophecy: "The Touch of Death"

71. Quoted in Drake, *Life of Tecumseh and of His Brother the Prophet*, p. 193.

72. Quoted in Drake, *Life of Tecumseh and of His Brother the Prophet*, p. 193.

73. Quoted in Hook, *Tecumseh: Visionary Chief of the Shawnee*, p. 42.

74. Quoted in Norman Donaldson and Betty Donaldson, *How Did They Die?* New York: St. Martin's Press, 1980, pp. 356–57.

75. Quoted in Donaldson and Donaldson, *How Did They Die?*, pp. 356–57.

76. Quoted in Hook, *Tecumseh: Visionary Chief of the Shawnee*, p. 42.

77. Quoted in Hook, *Tecumseh: Visionary Chief of the Shawnee*, p. 44.

78. Quoted in Hook, *Tecumseh: Visionary Chief of the Shawnee*, p. 43.

79. Quoted in Hook, *Tecumseh: Visionary Chief of the Shawnee*, p. 44.

80. Quoted in McGovern, *The Defenders*, p. 90.

For Further Reading

Jane Fleischer, *Tecumseh: Shawnee War Chief.* Mahwah, NJ: Troll Associates, 1979. Straightforward, easy-to-read story of the life of Tecumseh.

Zachery Kent, *Tecumseh.* Chicago: Childrens Press, 1992. Tells the story of Tecumseh in an interesting and easy-to-follow way.

Russell Shorto, *Tecumseh and the Dream of an American Indian Nation.* Englewood Cliffs, NJ: Silver Burdett, 1989. Plain talk about Tecumseh and his hopes and dreams for his people.

James Alexander Thom, *Panther in the Sky.* New York: Ballantine Books, 1990. Exciting historical novel, written so well that it makes Tecumseh, the Shawnee, and the life and events of the time come alive.

Timothy Truman, *Allan W. Eckert's Tecumseh: An Illustrated Adaptation.* Forestville, CA: Eclipse Books, 1992. Great fun—a comic book all about Tecumseh.

Works Consulted

William Jackson Armstrong, *The Heroes of Defeat.* Cincinnati, OH: Robert Clarke, 1905. Flowery, intellectual treatise on six "heroes," one of whom is Tecumseh, the author's "Hero of the Forest."

William Atkinson, *The Next New Madrid Earthquake: A Survival Guide for the Midwest.* Carbondale and Edwardsville: Southern Illinois University Press, 1989. In-depth discussion of the past, present, and future earthquakes, with the focus on the 1811 earthquake predicted by Tecumseh.

John Bennett, *Blue Jacket: War Chief of the Shawnees.* Chillicothe, OH: Ross County Historical Society Press, 1943. Booklet basically devoted to Blue Jacket, which does include some interesting anecdotes and revelations about Tecumseh.

Peter I. Bosco, *The War of 1812.* Brookfield, CT: Millbrook Press, 1991. Offers good explanation of what led to the war and describes the events of the war itself and the people who took part in it.

Kate Connell, *These Lands Are Ours: Tecumseh's Fight for the Old Northwest.* Austin, TX: Steck-Vaughn/Raintree, 1993. Simplified version of the life of Tecumseh.

Luella Sanders Bruce Creighton, *Tecumseh: The Story of the Shawnee Chief.* Toronto: Macmillan, 1965. Part of the Great Stories of Canada series. Account of the life of Tecumseh from birth to death written in story form to appeal to a young audience.

Norman Donaldson and Betty Donaldson, *How Did They Die?* New York: St. Martin's Press, 1980. Series of interesting accounts of the events and commentaries surrounding the deaths of a number of important individuals.

Benjamin Drake, *The Life of Tecumseh and of His Brother the Prophet; with a Historical Sketch of the Shawanoe Indians.* 1858. Reprint Salem, NH: Ayer, 1988. Written in true nineteenth-century style; considered until recent years the definitive biography of Tecumseh.

Allan W. Eckert, *The Frontiersmen.* Boston: Little, Brown, 1967. First book in the Winning of America series. Dramatic history thoroughly researched and written in novel form. Interweaves the stories of Simon Kenton, Daniel Boone, and other heroes of the American frontier, wilderness America, and Tecumseh and the grandeur and tragedy of his people.

———, *A Sorrow in Our Heart: The Life of Tecumseh.* New York: Bantam Books, 1992. Epic, massively researched biography of Tecumseh by a Pulitzer Prize–winning author. Clear, well documented, and written in narrative biography style. Captures not only the greatness of Tecumseh but the unsettling and changing times in which he lived.

R. David Edmunds, *The Shawnee Prophet.* Lincoln: University of Nebraska Press, 1983. An academic historian explores the lives, careers, and relationship of Tenskwatawa—the Prophet—and his brother Tecumseh. Takes the view that the Prophet, not Tecumseh, was the true visionary and leader.

John R. Etting, *Amateurs, to Arms! A Military History of the War of 1812*. Chapel Hill, NC: Algonquin Books of Chapel Hill, 1991. A military historian describes the military developments of America's "Second War of Independence" and shows how the war was fought and lost.

John Fleischman, "Tecumseh's New Take," *Ohio*, May 1994. Tells why and in what ways Tecumseh generates discussions and interest and is represented in the theater and in print today.

Chuck Fulkerson, *Native American People: The Shawnee*. Vero Beach, FL: Rourke, 1992. Easy-to-read introduction to the Shawnee culture, beliefs, way of life, and leaders.

Jason Hook, *Tecumseh: Visionary Chief of the Shawnee*. Dorset, UK: Firebird Books, 1989. Part of the Heroes and Warriors Series; clearly pro-Tecumseh discussion, interspersed with primary sources, of the Shawnee leader's life and philosophy.

Joseph Bryan Icenhower, *Tecumseh and the Indian Confederation, 1811–1813: The Indian Nations East of the Mississippi Are Defeated*. New York: Franklin Watts, 1975. Straight historical account that focuses on the major events in Tecumseh's life.

Carl Frederick Klinck, *Tecumseh: Fact and Fiction in Early Records*. Englewood Cliffs, NJ: Prentice-Hall, 1961. Collection of letters, reports, historical accounts, reminiscences, and descriptions by people who actually knew Tecumseh; taken from early Canadian and American sources.

Robert Leckie, *The Wars of America*. New York: Harper & Row, 1968. Account of different wars in which the United States was involved.

Dumas Malone, ed., *Dictionary of American Biography*, vol. IX. New York: Charles Scribner's Sons, 1964. Reference work with entries arranged in alphabetical order. Provides interesting biographical summaries about individuals from different periods of history.

Albert Marrin, *1812: The War Nobody Won*. New York: Atheneum, 1985. Discussion of the war and Tecumseh's role in it, with primary sources interwoven.

James McCague, *Tecumseh: Shawnee Warrior-Statesman*. Champaign, IL: Garrard, 1970. Easy-to-read story about the life of Tecumseh, from his early childhood to his death.

John McDonald, "General Simon Kenton," *Biographical Sketches of General Nathaniel Massie, General Duncan McArthur, Captain William Wells, and General Simon Kenton*. Cincinnati, OH: E. Morgan, 1838. Interesting nineteenth-century portrait of the life and times of the frontiersman whose path crossed that of Tecumseh more than once.

Ann McGovern, *The Defenders*. London: Scholastic Book Services, 1970. Stories about three Native American leaders—the Seminole Osceola, the Apache Cochise, and the Shawnee Tecumseh—who tried to protect the right of their people to stay on land that had been theirs long before the white settlers came.

Thomas L. McKenney and James Hall, Esq., *History of the Indian Tribes of North America with Biographical Sketches and*

Anecdotes of the Principal Chiefs, vol. II. 1842. Reprint Kent, OH: Volair Limited, 1978. Written in the language of the time and reflecting the attitudes and biases of the era. Provides background and interesting information about Native American leaders. Illustrated with 120 portraits from the Department of War's Indian Gallery.

Warren King Moorehead, *The Indian Tribes of Ohio Historically Considered: A Preliminary Paper*. 1899. Reprint n.d., New York: AMS Press, for the Ohio State Archaeological and Historical Society by Fred J. Heer. Documented study that includes many references from the work of Benjamin Drake.

Elizabeth Eggleston Seelye, *Tecumseh and the Shawnee Prophet*. New York: Dodd, Mead, 1878. Detailed account of Tecumseh and of his brother, written in the stilted style of the 1800s and reflecting the prejudices of that time.

Lloyd Emerson Siberell, *Tecumseh: His Career, the Man, His Chillicothe Portrait*. Chillicothe, OH: Ross County Historical Society, 1944. Small booklet that describes Tecumseh and his career, discusses the famous Chillicothe portrait of him, and provides a transcript and reproduction of a letter about him.

William H. Van Hoose, *Tecumseh: An Indian Moses*. Canton, OH: Daring Books, 1984. Biography that puts Tecumseh and his life squarely in the perspective of his times, emphasizing the events and ways of life that characterized the period.

Laura Pienkny Zakin, "The Passing of a People," *Columbus Monthly*, July 1993. Background and descriptions of Logan, Tarhe, Leatherlips, and Tecumseh—Indian leaders who tried to save their people's lands in central Ohio.

Index

Picture Credits

Cover photo: Stock Montage, Inc.

The American Revolution: A Picture Sourcebook by Dover Publications, Inc., 22, 36

The Bettmann Archive, 42, 89

Brown Brothers, 32

Corbis-Bettmann, 27, 74, 96

Culver Pictures, Inc., 62, 64, 92

Department of Canadian Heritage: Fort Malden National Historic Site, 71 (a view of Amherstburg, 1813, by Margaret Reynolds); 86 (General Henry Proctor, by J. C. H. Forster)

Library of Congress, 11, 15, 16, 19, 20, 21, 34, 45, 48, 53, 63, 65, 69, 76, 81, 85, 88, 95

National Archives, 99

National Museum of American Art, Washington DC/Art Resource, NY, 50

National Portrait Gallery, Smithsonian Institution/Art Resource, NY, 44, 75, 82

North Wind Picture Archives, 10, 47, 59, 78, 84

Peter Newark's Western Americana, 38, 67

Stock Montage, Inc., 29, 30, 35, 55

About the Authors

Myra H. and William H. Immell did their undergraduate study at Ohio University. Myra also attended the Universidad de Madrid and Rutgers University. She taught Spanish and English as a second language for a number of years. For more than twenty years, she was associated with Merrill Publishing Company, where her primary involvement was with educational materials. For two years, she was director of high school programs for Quest International, a nonprofit organization that promotes positive youth development. This is the second book she has written for Lucent. William is a certified public accountant in private practice. A native of Chillicothe, Ohio, his avocation is U.S. history. This is the first book he has written. The Immells live in a suburb of Columbus, Ohio, in the heart of Shawnee country.